A FRIENDLY GUIDE TO THE MASS

TONY DOHERTY

johngarrattpublishing

Published by
John Garratt Publishing
32 Glenvale Crescent
Mulgrave Vic 3170
www.johngarratt.com.au

Copyright © 2010 Tony Doherty

All rights reserved. Except as provided by the Australian copyright law, no part of this book may be reproduced in any way without permission in writing fom the publisher.

Design and typesetting by Lynne Muir
Text editing by Ann M Phillpot

Cataloguing-in-publication information for this title is available from the National Library of Australia.
www.nla.gov.au

ISBN 9781920721954

Nihil Obstat: Reverend Gerard Diamond MA (Oxon), LSS, D Theol
Diocesan Censor
Imprimatur Most Reverend Les Tomlinson DD
Titular Bishop of Siniti, Vicar General
Date 26th August 2010

The Nihil Obstat and Imprimatur are official declarations that a book or pamphlet is free of doctrinal or moral error. No implication is contained therein that those who have granted the Nihil Obstat and Imprimatur agree with the contents, opinions or statements expressed. They do not necessarily signify that the work is approved as a basic text for catechetical instruction.

"Song of the Body of Christ" by David Haas
Copyright © 1989 by GIA Publications, Inc.,
7404 S. Mason Ave., Chicago, IL 60638
www.giamusic.com 800.442.1358
All rights reserved. Used by permission.

Scripture quotations are drawn from the *New Revised Standard Version of the Bible*, copyright ©1989 by the Division of Christian Education of the National Council of the Churches of Christ in the USA. Used by permission. All rights reserved.

References

Bach, Richard, *Jonathan Livingstone Seagull*, Avon Books, New York, 1970.
Catechism of the Catholic Church, St Pauls Press, Homebush, 1995.
Chittister, Joan, *In search of belief*, Harper Collins Publishers, Melbourne, 1999.
Covey, Stephen, *The 7 habits of highly effective people*, Simon and Schuster, New York, 1990.
Doyle, Brian, *Leaping revelations and epiphanies*, Loyola Press, Chicago, 2003.
Edwards, Denis, *Ecology at the heart of faith*, Orbis Books, Maryknoll, New York, 2006.
Martel, Yann, *The Life of Pi*, Harcourt, New York, 2001.
Newman, J H, *Parochial and Plain Sermons*, Longmans, Green & Co, London, 1907.
Nouwen, Henri, *Clowning in Rome*, Seabury Press, New York, 1978.
O'Leary, Daniel, *Prism of love*, Columba Press, Blackrock, Dublin, 2003.
Pope Benedict XVI, *Spe Salvi*, Encyclical Letter, 2007.
Radcliffe, Timothy, *Why go to church*, Continuum, London, 2008.

Photo credits:

Photographs on cover by Peter Casamento, iStockphoto and Taizé
Photographs on pages 8, 11, 12, 17, 20, 22, 25, 30, 31, 32, 33, 34, 35, 36, 37, 38, 40, 44, 48, 54, 56, 57, 63, 64 by Peter Casamento; on pages 5, 26, 31, 34, 41, 45, 47 from iStockphoto; on pages 4, 6, 7, 15, 18, 27, 49, 50, 52, 53, 59, 61, 64 by Lynne Muir; on page.31 by Susan Daily; on page 62 by Sabine Leutenegger, ©Ateliers et Presses de Taizé, 71250 Taizé, France.
Photograph on p39 'Earthrise – Apollo 8' from NASA http://grin.hq.nasa.gov/ABSTRACTS/GPN-2001-000009.html

Contents

Preface
Capturing the mystery in words   5

The Introductory Rite
The dreams of a celebrant   8
An early description of the Mass   12
The different parts of the Mass   13
Confessing our sins   15

The Liturgy of the Word
Listening to the sacred scriptures   18
Listening to the Old Testament   20
Listening to the Gospel   22
The creed   26

A short history of the Mass   31
The Prayers of the Faithful   35

The Liturgy of the Eucharist
Preparing the bread and the wine   38
The central prayer of the Eucharist   41
A community gathered here   44
The Sign of Peace   48
Holy Communion   50
Time for Thanksgiving   52

The Concluding Rite
The Mass is ended – go in peace   56

Appendices
The Eucharist in Scripture   60
Music in the Mass   62
Catechism of the Catholic Church – texts   63

Preface
Capturing the mystery in words

After celebrating Mass each day for close to fifty years, there is something a little uncomfortable about being asked to capture in words what has become as familiar to you as eating and sleeping. It leaves you with a feeling of disquiet, like being asked to submit your own mother to psychological analysis.

How do you explain a mystery? What does the Eucharist really mean? What is going on in the minds of those gathered at a normal Sunday parish Mass? A more daunting question would be what would it look like if people really participated fully in the Mass, acting in a manner unlike that of being passive spectators? Or, even, how often should it be celebrated? Or, simply, what should it be called?

There are so many facets to the diamond. For some it is a meal. For some it is a sacrifice. Others experience it as a bit of both, a 'sacrifice-meal'. For some it is a ritual act, sacred and set apart. Others like to emphasise the community aspect – the community gathering together, very conscious of one another. For some it is a deeply personal prayer. For others it is a sacramental celebration embracing the entire world.

For some its very essence is expressed in the coming together (the communion) of those present. While for others, the driving force of the prayer nourishes a deep-seated desire to reach out to some wider group. Like the memory of Jesus washing the feet of his young friends, the Mass contains a challenge, for these people, to wash the feet of the lonely and those broken on life's journey. For some, it is a celebration of a death on Calvary, in which they may find a poignant echo of the grief and distress within their own lives. For others, it is the moment to celebrate the sacredness of life in joy and gratitude. Some celebrate it once a year. Others celebrate it four times a year. Some celebrate it every Sunday and for others it is a daily event of thanksgiving and grace.

For some worshippers it is a celebration of a reconciliation which forgives and unites. For others, unity and reconciliation are pre-requisites for its proper celebration. Some call it the Lord's Supper; others call it the Holy Sacrifice of the Mass; still others call it the Eucharist. Most commonly, Catholics use the shorthand word with which they are most comfortable, simply 'the Mass'.

Even the elements of bread and wine at its centre are not quite as uncomplicated as they may seem. The presence of a small wafer and a cup of wine in its simplicity disguise many hidden depths of meaning. There are few domestic delights (for some at least) that match the impact of fresh bread – the aroma and shape of a new steaming loaf coming out of an oven in the early morning. Bread can carry the nostalgic memory of a family table. Breaking the bread has become a symbol of the very act of sharing life itself. And yet, on the other hand, the creation of a loaf of bread destroys much in the making – the crushing of grains of wheat, the

milling of flour, the baking in the intense heat of a fire. Many grains are crushed into one loaf. The very existence of bread is made possible from the destruction of the grain.

And the wine. For countless ages, wine has been a symbol of companionship and human celebration, of weddings and family joy – an ancient elixir designed to lift the spirit and add to the vitality of life itself. Yet, even wine has its darker side. It is created from grapes pulped in a crusher, pressed down and destroyed in the making, left to mature in subterranean containers. In the Eucharist, the crushing of grapes serve as a sober reminder of the blood of Jesus poured out in death, his broken body laid in a grave. It also reminds us of those crushed in the sometimes bitter reality of living or merely surviving in this broken world. It is no wonder that these seemingly uncomplicated gifts of bread and wine have become stark reminders of a powerful symbolism of the hope of new life rising out of death – the central message of the Gospel, which presents us with the story of Christ undergoing his own death and being raised by his Father to a new risen life.

Where do we stop? Who is right? The Eucharist is all of these things and more. It is rather like a majestic river gum standing at the side of a drought-threatened stream. As the day draws to a close, the towering eucalypt catches the rays of the sun in the ever-changing angles of its glistening leaves. Its many branches are an image of the many layers embraced within the meaning of the Mass, the variety of its many rituals, and the centuries of worshippers from every age and corner of the planet that it has gathered in its embrace. Its hidden roots, thrusting into the river bank, suggest the story of liberation and freedom from slavery embedded in its Jewish past, which hold the central trunk strong and stable.

So I invite you to come and climb this giant tree. Don't be afraid. There will be branches to rest in, shade to cover you and panoramic views to delight you. This book contains an invitation to ascend this tree and explore this view like a curious child, finding in its branches a place to dream and a vantage point to recognise the astonishing gift given to those of us who share the ancient tradition which we call our Mass.

The introductory rite
The dreams of a celebrant

Saturday night. 6 p.m. The parish Mass begins in a simple suburban church. The small group of people greet the priest with the opening song:

We come to share our story.
We come to break the bread.
We come to know our rising from the dead.

The celebrant makes his way to the church sanctuary, kisses the altar and turns to greet this little band of believers scattered through the dimly lit church. He reflects on the words of the hymn "We come to share our story…". *If only we could share our story*, he muses. *If only we had the space and the time to share the real experiences of what is happening in our lives.*

If only we had the trust and confidence in one another to share the secrets of our fragile hearts. The practical voice within him insists – stop dreaming and get on with Mass.

And yet, each of the people there – the lonely and the bruised, the shy and the poised, the fragile and the strong – have their own stories. They each have their own hungers and their own dreams. *What a parish family could be built if we had the trusting hearts to open ourselves up to others, and then to listen to the stories of frustration and delight, of boredom and of joy, of grief and endless discovery!*

Helen living alone now – widowed for the last fifteen years. At Mass each morning. Susie, a thirty-something gym instructor, restless and searching. She aches to settle down and marry. But it hasn't worked out…yet. Jonathan and Mari from Malaysia, emotionally bleeding about their son's crippling financial debts – and they don't know how best to help him. Debbie who gave birth to her first child three weeks ago, lights up the pew with the distinctive glow of a new mother, in need of a little sleep but alive and well. Lenka and Jurek recently arrived from a Polish winter in Krakow. Can't understand English but feel strangely at home within the familiar rhythm of the ritual. Andy, he must be fifteen by now, struggling with his new high school, quiet and a little too reserved for his boisterous classmates.

And dozens of others, all with their own story – some lifetime believers, some half-believers, others once-upon-a-time-believers but still strangely curious. A sprinkling of those attending are not even Catholic but may come from an Anglican or Uniting Church tradition. Even a couple of Buddhists may be in attendance. Nothing abnormal – just another Sunday congregation; the priest is quite used to it.

Jonathan Livingstone Seagull was a best-selling book which told the story of a seabird feeling deeply dissatisfied with life, restless for wider horizons and a broader sky to explore. This powerful little parable, of the hunger within each person to search and explore life more fully, still touches deep-down nerves in contemporary audiences. Strong parables contain a certain ageless genius.

The little seagull's hunger finds an echo in the restless spirit within each one of us. Thousands

8 A Friendly Guide to the Mass

of readers still identify closely with that itch. Their life journey, they feel, has lost some of its music. The dreams they once cherished have become domesticated. The lonely little seagull has found a nest in their hearts.

Looking around the church, the priest asks himself – *what are these faithful people gathered in this church really searching for? And more to the point, how can he break open the Eucharist and offer them food to nourish their searching spirits and strengthen them on their sometimes frustrating but often courageous journey?*

> *We are called to heal the broken,*
> *to be hope for the poor*
> *we are called to feed the hungry at our door.*

Life contains both its prose and its poetry. This ancient celebration of Mass, the celebrant believes, is the brilliantly simple sacrament which brings life's prose and its poetry into balance. The everyday stuff of life is the prose – the grinding obligations of work; the ambiguity of human friendship; the constant responsibility for other family members; the aches and pains of an ageing body; the compulsions and addictions of a consumer society.

And yet the poetry of this age-old Catholic faith of ours holds the belief that we are immersed in mystery, that our lives are more than they seem, that we belong to each other and to a swirling universe whose energy resides in an ever-present, creator God.

> *Bread of life and cup of promise*
> *In this meal we all are one*
> *In our dying and in our rising*
> *May your kingdom come.*

Clearing his throat, the celebrant intones:

> *In the name of the Father and of the Son and of the Holy Spirit…*

We come to share our story.
We come to break the bread.
We come to know our rising from the dead.

We are called to heal the broken,
to be hope for the poor
we are called to feed the hungry at our door.

Bread of life and cup of promise
In this meal we all are one
In our dying and in our rising
May your kingdom come.

from "Song of the Body of Christ" by David Haas

Did You Know

Some things about the Mass

- Catholics go to Mass on Sundays because they believe it is central to their lives as Christians.

- Sunday was the day the Father raised Jesus from the dead.

- Jesus is really present in the Eucharist. A believer receives the body and blood of Christ under the form of bread and wine, which we call Holy Communion.

- At times, for practical reasons, communion is simply offered under the form of bread.

- The Mass can be understood to have two parts – the readings from the Bible (called the Liturgy of the Word) and the prayer over the bread and wine (called the Liturgy of the Eucharist). This Eucharist is then shared among those who attend the Mass.

- Bells are rung to indicate important moments in the Eucharist.

- The first part of the Mass (the Liturgy of the Word) is based on the ancient Jewish synagogue service.

- The second part of Mass (the Liturgy of the Eucharist) is based on our understanding of what happened at the Last Supper.

- Many ancient cathedrals are designed to have the Mass celebrated on an altar far removed from the people – to emphasise the mystery that is being enacted.

- In some Eastern churches, for the same reason, the Eucharistic Prayer even takes place behind a screen hidden from the people.

- Now, more frequently, the altar is placed in the centre of the church or, at least, closer to the people in order to emphasise the crucial role of the people of God in the celebration.

- Following the Second Vatican Council's movement for renewal of the way Catholics pray, the Mass began to be celebrated with the priest facing the people. This was a return to the most ancient tradition.

- Catholics use unleavened bread (without yeast) for the Eucharist but most Eastern churches use leavened bread.

The Sign of the Cross

No other simple physical gesture is so widespread among Catholics as this sign.

Life's experiences, great and small, holy and horrendous, are marked by this handmade echo of the crucifixion. As men and women who believe in the Risen Christ, the God and man who died on a wooden cross long centuries ago, we use this sign. Scholars trace the practice as far back as the year 110, by which time it was already established as a common gesture among Christians – most common, apparently, among those Christian communities associated with St Paul. It is a small miracle, perhaps, that this gesture has persisted unchanged throughout many centuries and many cultures.

Simple, powerful, poignant, the Sign of the Cross is an action like the Mass, in which we sit down to table fellowship with one another and remember the Last Supper, or a baptism, where we remember John the Baptist pouring water from the river Jordan over Jesus, his cousin.

As believers enter a church, they take water and bless themselves, which becomes an uncomplicated and potent reminder of the implications of being a baptised person.

"Such a ferocious and brave notion," remarks American essayist Brian Doyle, "to be hinted at by such a simple motion, and the gesture lasting perhaps all of four seconds, if you touch all the bases and don't rush. But as simple as the Sign of the Cross is, it carries a brave weight: it names the Trinity, celebrates the Creator, and brings home all the power of faith to the brush of fingers in skin and bone and belly."

A sign which helps us to remember that we have a 'companion' on the road.

An early description of the Mass

Around the year 155, an early Christian philosopher, Justin Martyr wrote an open letter to the Roman Emperor Antoninus Pius to explain what Christians did:

On the day we call the day of the sun, all who dwell in the city or the country gather in the same place.

The memoirs of the apostles and the writings of the prophets are read, as much as time permits.

When the reader has finished, he who presides over those gathered admonishes and challenges them to imitate these beautiful things.

Then we all rise together and offer prayers for ourselves…and for all others, wherever they may be, so that we may be found righteous by our life and actions, and faithful to the commandments, so as to obtain eternal salvation.

When the prayers are concluded we exchange the kiss.

Then someone brings bread and a cup of water and wine mixed together to him who presides over the brethren.

He takes them and offers praise and glory to the Father of the universe, through the name of the Son and of the Holy Spirit, and for a considerable time he gives thanks that we have been judged worthy of these gifts.

When he has concluded the prayers and thanksgivings, all present give voice to the acclamation by saying: 'Amen'.

When he who presides has given thanks and the people have responded, those whom we call deacons give to those present the 'eucharisted' bread, wine and water and take them to those who are absent.

Catechism of the Catholic Church, 1345

The different parts of the Mass

INTRODUCTORY RITES

Entrance Procession
Greeting
Penitential Act
Glory be to God
Opening Prayer

LITURGY OF THE WORD

First Reading
Psalm
Second Reading
Gospel Acclamation
Gospel
Homily
The Creed
Prayers of the Faithful

LITURGY OF THE EUCHARIST

Offertory
The Eucharistic Prayer
Preface
Holy, Holy
Memorial Acclamation

Communion Rite
The Lord's Prayer – Our Father
Sign of Peace
Lamb of God
Holy Communion
Prayer after Communion

CONCLUDING RITES

Final Blessing
The Dismissal

Did You Know

The Sacrament of many names

- **The Eucharist** – because it is an action of thanksgiving. The Greek word for giving thanks *eucharistein* recalls, especially during a meal, the Jewish blessings that proclaim God's works of creation, redemption and sanctification.

- **The Lord's Supper** – because of its connection with the meal which the Lord took with his disciples on the eve of his Passion.

- **The breaking of the bread** – because Jesus used this ritual when, as master of the table, he blessed and distributed the bread at the Last Supper. The disciples will recognise him immediately in this characteristic action after his Resurrection. It is the earliest term, used by the first Christians, to describe their coming together 'in memory of Jesus'.

- **The Eucharistic Assembly** – because the Eucharist is celebrated amid a gathering of believers. It is the visible expression of the Church itself.

- **The Memorial of the Lord's Passion and Resurrection** – because the night before he died, Jesus asked us to do this in memory of him.

- **The Holy Sacrifice** – because it makes present the sacrifice Christ the Saviour made at Calvary. The terms 'Holy Sacrifice of the Mass', 'Sacrifice of Praise', 'Spiritual Sacrifice' are also used.

- **The Holy Liturgy** – because the Church's whole liturgy finds its centre and most intense expression in the celebration of this sacrament. In the same sense, we also call its enactment the 'Celebration of the Sacred Mysteries'. We speak of the 'Most Blessed Sacrament' because it is the Sacrament of sacraments.

- **Holy Communion** – because by this sacrament we unite ourselves to Christ, who makes us sharers in his body and blood to form a single body.

- **The Mass** or **Holy Mass** – because the liturgy concludes with the people being 'sent forth', so that they may live out the Christian ideal in their daily lives. It also refers to the practice of the Eucharist (Holy Communion) being taken to those who are sick or unable to come to church. ('Mass' comes from the Latin words *missa est*, which can be broadly translated as 'you are sent forth' or 'it is sent forth'.)

ABRIDGED FROM THE CATECHISM OF THE CATHOLIC CHURCH

Confessing our sins
Searching for who we really are

"Going to church no more makes you a Christian than sleeping in a garage makes you a car" goes an old saying.

"Well," we might ask, "What *does* make one a Christian?"

To be a Christian, from the very beginning, surely is to respond to an invitation – neither more nor less – to be part of a community which makes an honest effort to live by the values of the Gospel. And it doesn't take long to realise, with some pain, that you knock over a lot of hurdles on the track as you struggle to persevere in the long distance race undertaken by the believing person.

The process is as bumpy as an outback dirt road damaged by heavy rain.

"Most of our tears begin to flow when we see the difference between the dreams we once had for our lives and the way we have turned out to be" goes another saying. To confront ourselves with our dark side may seem a gloomy way to start a celebration. It may appear as if to be welcomed to the feast, we must first feel bad about ourselves. But it is not quite like that.

There are some confusing notions of forgiveness and sin even among quite experienced Catholics. When God forgives sin, there is no change in God's mind about us. It is our mind that changes about God. You see, the most ancient Catholic belief is that we have an unchanging God. In the various acts of reconciliation, it is we who change. Our mind comes to realise the dimension of God's unconditional love directed towards us. If we go to confession, it is not to plead for forgiveness from God, but to welcome God's offer and thank God for it.

"God cannot remember our sins," Irish writer Daniel O'Leary keenly observes, "or forget our beauty." We are always caught up in the extravagant love of a gentle and gracious God. O'Leary says, "We are utterly divine and we do not know it; we are full of God's loveliness and we don't believe it; we can heal each other, as Jesus did, but nobody told us."

Most sin is pretending to be someone else – someone smarter, someone more beautiful, someone more worthy of admiration. Often we live desperate for reassurance. "To sin is always to construct an illusory self that we can admire," Dominican Herbert McCabe observes, "instead of the real self that we can love."

There is an old Jewish story about the Rabbi Zusia who said, "When I shall face the celestial tribunal, I shall not be asked why I was not Abraham, Jacob or Moses. I shall be asked why I was not Zusia."

So right at the beginning of Mass, surrounded by the struggling souls in the pews around us, we are invited to confront ourselves calmly but honestly with the question which, like some elusive fish, swims just below the surface of the consciousness of each of us. Who am I, really?

Brothers and sisters, let us acknowledge our sins, and so prepare ourselves to celebrate the sacred mysteries.

Challenging that denial of responsibility, which is endemic in our contemporary world, the community replies:

Lord have mercy,
Christ have mercy,
Lord have mercy.

This cry from the people is so ancient that in a normal Latin Mass these words of petition are expressed in the Greek language used widely by the early Church:

Kyrie Eleison
Christe Eleison.

"An elderly English Catholic lost in Athens was unable to stop any taxis to take him back to his hotel, and was reduced to shouting to the taxi drivers the only Greek he knew, "*Kyrie Eleison* (Lord have mercy)," Dominican Timothy Radcliffe recalls. "Happily our hero found his taxi."

To be a Christian, then, is to have the courage to face oneself, the confidence to pray "Lord have mercy", and the liberating belief that we are loved unconditionally and without qualification by the God who breathed life into us in the first place.

So we enter the mystery of the Eucharist, simply and powerfully, by claiming our real selves in an act of genuine integrity and refusing to play-act some other identity which is mere illusion.

"Christianity is a freedom story," Australian writer Michael McGirr believes, "to release us from the tyranny of our own ego." And, we might add, that story is at its most powerful in the celebration of the Eucharist.

Most of our tears
begin to flow
when we see the difference
between the dreams
we once had for our lives
and the way we have
turned out to be.

The Liturgy of the Word

Listening to the Sacred Scriptures – Never Easy
Breaking open the Word of God

The Japanese word for 'too busy' is composed of two characters 'heart' and 'destruction'. Enough said. When we make ourselves so busy that we are rushing around trying to get this or that done, we kill something vital in ourselves and we smother the quiet wisdom of our heart. In the book of Ecclesiastes, there is a proverb:

Better one hand full of quiet than two hands full of striving after wind.

Unpractised in the art of quiet, we hope to find our safety, our belonging and our healing by raising the levels of hustle. But our frantic busyness actually makes us deaf to what is healing and sacred both in ourselves and in others. "It is not enough to be busy," says Thoreau, "So are ants. What is important is what we are busy about."

At the beginning of Mass, we are invited to slow down and open our hearts to the Word of God – it is rarely an easy task. There would be very few people who do not face a problem in just listening intelligently to the biblical readings at Mass.

We are invited to step back across the centuries, sometimes over twenty-five centuries and enter into the minds and beliefs of others who lived in cultures entirely foreign to the world in which we live. To listen intelligently, we are asked to appreciate the concerns which shaped their lives, the metaphors and images which excited their imagination, and the notion of the divine which nourished their faith. A most challenging work!

And yet, to take the example just mentioned of the proverb from Ecclesiastes, it is sometimes astonishing how the ancient Word can bridge the chasms of the centuries and connect us to insights as fresh today as they were to the ancients thousands of years ago. At other times, it must be admitted, these writings we treasure as our sacred inheritance are as hard to decipher as a cryptic crossword.

Each Sunday, the Mass has three readings: the first from the Hebrew Scriptures (often called the Old Testament); the second from a book of the New Testament (other than one of the four gospels); and the third, a reading from one of the gospels themselves. These readings follow a three-year cycle, so that a significant selection of the entire Bible is read and reflected upon by the Mass-going community over these years.

The words of the Bible, strange to our modern ears at times, are a true love story between a people and their God. In the beginning, there existed a group of nomadic Hebrews who struggled to understand their destiny in history. The story gradually describes the development of a people coming to appreciate the promises of a God who would be faithful to them, come what may. And then, rising from these people, come the gospels of the early Christian movement, expressing the Good News which Jesus the Christ brought of God's continuing presence in their midst as 'the Risen Christ'.

Allow the words of this love story to engage the quiet wisdom of your hungry heart.

Did You Know

The Jewish Scriptures

- The Jewish Scriptures are often referred to as the Old Testament. These were the writings and traditions that were sacred for Jesus.

- They consist of 46 books composed between the eighth-century BC and the time of Jesus.

- The first five books of the Bible are known as the Pentateuch (*penta* is the Greek word for 'five') and they refer to the origins of life and of some of the primitive stories and events of the people of Israel.

- The first five books are Genesis, Exodus, Leviticus, Numbers and Deuteronomy.

- The word 'Testament' refers to a covenant or agreement God made with the Hebrew people, often expressed in the shorthand phrase "I will be your God and you will be my people".

- The Law, another sacred Hebrew responsibility, given by God to Moses, the leader of his people at the time, was Israel's obligation under the covenant.

- The Covenant and the Law define Hebrew identity and are the foundation of Hebrew life.

- The second collection of books in the Old Testament are the books of the prophets.

- 'Prophets' in this context refer to people who were inspired by God to alert the community of Israel to the presence and action of God in their midst.

- These books include the books of Joshua, Judges, 1 and 2 Samuel and 1 and 2 Kings. Some of the prophetic books are named after important prophets, for example, Isaiah, Jeremiah and Ezekiel.

- The third collection of books in the Old Testament include prayers (such as The Psalms), wisdom (such as Proverbs and Wisdom) and short stories (such as Jonah, Ruth and Judith).

- Readings from most of these books make up the first reading at Sunday Mass during the year.

LISTENING TO THE OLD TESTAMENT
The challenge of reading the Hebrew Scriptures

The little band of worshippers settled down in their seats to listen to the biblical readings for this particular Sunday. A grey-haired, comfortably dressed woman in her early fifties, Pauline, walked to the lectern and opened the book of readings. Prior to taking her turn at ministering to the community by reading at Mass, she has spent time pondering the following questions.

How do I read this very ancient text, with all of its unfamiliar and unusual language? she muses. *How am I able to present this reading with clarity and conviction so that these genuine and honest people will garner some meaning from it for their lives?*

The advice of the teacher at the course which prepared her for this moment came back to her.

Ask yourself – when did this writing take place?

The Hebrew Scriptures are a collection of books committed to writing during a period of time spread over many hundreds of years. And very often the books were not the product of a single effort. Some of them only took shape gradually. The book of Deuteronomy is a typical example. It is interspersed with laws dating from many different eras. It was a code that grew along with the people. The Psalms is another book that took centuries to develop fully. Between the oldest and the most recent psalms is an interval of eight hundred years. These books, which were the sacred stories which formed Jesus as a young person, reflected the whole long story of the Hebrew people.

This Sunday's first reading, Pauline recognised, was the call of Jeremiah to be a prophet.

*"Before I formed you in the womb I knew you,
and before you were born I consecrated you;
I appointed you a prophet of the nations."*

*Then I said, "Ah, Lord God!
Truly I do not know how to speak,
for I am only a boy." (Jeremiah 1:5, 6)*

She recalled the pattern of 'the reluctant prophet' that ran throughout so many Jewish stories of the past. The response of Jeremiah, that he was not up to the task being asked of him, echoed the lives of many past Jewish leaders – Abraham, Moses, Samuel, Isaiah and the classic tale of Jonah (which rabbis used to love to tell – they probably still do!), which describes the lengths to which he went to evade God's invitation to be a prophet. He jumped into a boat to avoid the call, was hit by a cyclonic storm at sea, and, by courtesy of a whale (a large fish, actually), was deposited on the very shore of the country he was being asked to challenge.

The responses from the reluctant prophets can be summed up as:

*Please, leave me alone.
I don't want to speak to you.
I'm not worthy.
I am too young (or too old).
I can't do it.
Try someone else.*

Sounded familiar, even to Pauline herself, when she remembered the moment the parish council chair approached her about becoming a reader. Perhaps it's part of the story of each one of us!

In each of these cases, after a variety of personal struggles, the final response was

Here I am, Lord. (the words of a much loved hymn)

Finally, each accepts the challenge to travel with their gracious God into an unknown future.

It is never easy to travel from today's

post-modern, fast-tracked, mobile-phone civilisation back to the faraway culture and concerns of the society that gave birth to the Bible. But the enduring wisdom of our ancient Church invites us to take that journey every Sunday. The sacred scriptures have a hidden seam of precious metal, which it is our task to carefully uncover – the evolving story of God's passion for the human adventure, the gradual tale of God's friendship and faithfulness to humanity. We begin to glimpse who we are and where we are headed; and how we are being gently called into the future by a faithful God.

Perhaps the best advice is simply to listen. Stay with the story, rest in its presence, not trying too hard to understand it, but with open hearts treasuring this ancient Word as the account of a faithful God bringing life itself and its meaning to people.

Thomas Merton, the Cistercian monk, speaks of "the darkness of my empty mind, this sea that opens within me as soon as I close my eyes". Receive the Word with a quiet hospitality, and wait for the guest to open up to you.

Yann Martel writes in his novel *The Life of Pi*:

No thundering from a pulpit, no condemnation from bad churches, no peer pressure, just a book of scriptures quietly waiting to say hello, as gentle and powerful as a little girl's kiss on your cheek.

Did You Know

Paul the apostle

- The earliest written document in the New Testament, is believed to be Paul's letter to the Christian community in Thessalonika (in present-day Greece).

- There is a strong consensus among scripture scholars that, of the thirteen letters attributed to St Paul, he was the author of only seven.

- In approximate chronological order, they were The First Letter of Paul to the Thessalonians, The Letter of Paul to the Galatians, The First and Second Letter of Paul to the Corinthians, The Letter of Paul to the Philippians, The Letter of Paul to Philemon and The Letter of Paul to the Romans.

- All these letters were written in the fifties of the first century. The four Gospels of Mark, Matthew, Luke and John were therefore written later than St Paul's letters.

- The authorship of another three letters is disputed, but most agree that they were written not by Paul, but in his name after his death – The Letter of Paul to the Ephesians, The Letter of Paul to the Colossians and The Second Letter of Paul to the Thessalonians.

- Called the Pastoral Epistles, the remaining three letters were not written by Paul – first and second Timothy, and Titus.

- The decisive event in Paul's life was his experience of the Risen Christ on the road to Damascus, believed to be about the year 35.

- That experience transformed Paul. Before Damascus he was a zealous persecutor of the Jesus movement; afterwards, he became its foremost apostle.

Listening to the Gospel
Sharing stories around a flickering candle

The third-floor apartment was tiny. Bachelor-flat small. That was the price Christopher paid for living not too far from his city job. There were five of them cosily gathered around a table, simply decorated with a squat candle, a single flower and a copy of the New Testament.

Two couples and their host (the bachelor) had been meeting for two years now for a few weeks during the season of Lent to break open and discuss the gospel reading of the approaching Sunday. What *did* the Gospel have to say about their own struggles and dreams? What light and comfort *can* the Gospel bring to adults trying to make sense of their life in such turbulent times? In practical terms, just what *does* being a Catholic Christian really mean? These were all questions that stimulated serious consideration.

There was a quiet intimacy hearing the Gospel read over the crumbs of a just completed meal – a powerful echo of some other community of faith in a time long past. Often the words were familiar, yet certain phrases and images were strangely fresh as though heard for the first time.

Feeling comfortable and satisfied that they had grasped the essence of what was being read was rare. After all, Christopher reminded them, these writings were brought together two thousand years ago in an entirely different world, in an ancient language far removed from our time. Yet, with all of that distance, listening to what the Gospel stirred in the imagination of each in this small group left them at times with a feeling of being deeply and quietly nourished.

The gospels contain the stories of the first Christian believers – even before they were conscious of the term Christian. They were simply known as the 'followers of the Way'. Before the gospel writers – Matthew, Mark, Luke and John – fashioned their own contributions, these stories of faith were told and retold by those who first experienced the Risen Christ. Like so many other beliefs, Christianity was a faith built on experiences that were told in stories.

Following the ancient traditions of the classic Jewish teacher, Jesus shared his vision of life in the beguiling parable form, simple at first glance but never easily grasped in its entire meaning. He wove his teaching around stories of past heroes – Abraham, Isaac and David. In Jesus' words and phrases, the poetry of Isaiah and the psalmist are continually employed to illuminate Jesus' relationship to his Father, and to the vision of God's reign in our lives (which he called the 'kingdom of God' or the 'kingdom of heaven'). Jesus, the storyteller, lived with a fine appreciation that "we are made of stories".

Tonight's story from the gospels, which occupied the attention of Christopher and his friends, was the shadowy event of the meeting between the young teacher from Galilee and the uncertain rabbi called Nicodemus. "He came at night," the Gospel of John tells us.

One of the characteristics of John's gospel, is that it is populated with fairly seasoned adults wrestling with the tantalising questions which arise on the human journey. "A person is not old," the poet says, "as long as he or she is still seeking

22 A Friendly Guide to the Mass

something." John's gospel is crowded with searchers – troubled searchers, perhaps – but people who were gnawing on life's gristle, hungry for meaning and love.

Nicodemus, who faces his own unique demons; the Samaritan woman, thirsting for the water of a loving, faithful, adult relationship; the cruelly disabled man, waiting at the pool for thirty-eight years; the unnamed woman caught in adultery; the grieving sisters, Martha and Mary, dealing with the death of their brother – these are just some of the people we meet in John's gospel. They are *real* people facing *real* life. Few contemporary believers fail to find some echo in their own lives of similar challenges and questions.

The richness of the four gospels is that they each carry their own individual colour and purpose.

Matthew seems intent on emphasising to his own particular audience the Jewishness of Jesus: Jesus was the 'new' Moses who would go to the mountain and bring his people the new law of the beatitudes; like Moses, the infant Jesus would "come out of Egypt"; at Mount Tabor, Jesus is transfigured in the mysterious presence of Moses. Some even believe that the gospel itself is divided into five sections to reflect the five books of the Torah (the first books of the Bible), which are traditionally associated with Moses.

The Gospel of Mark, believed today to be the first gospel committed to writing, begins not with the stories of the birth and childhood of Jesus, but with the beginning of his ministry as an adult and his baptism by John the Baptist. On the other hand, the Gospels of Luke and Matthew describe the birth of Jesus at Bethlehem. Luke describes the mystery surrounding the announcement of Jesus' birth in one of the most moving descriptions in the New Testament: after being visited by an angel, Mary accepts the astonishing news of her role in the unfolding story of salvation. On the other hand, Matthew approaches the story through the troubled Joseph and his dreams, the designs of an evil king and the flight of the holy family into Egypt.

The gospels of Mark, Matthew and Luke, while differing in approach and perspective, have clear similarities, even to the extent of having many identical sections.

A cursory glance at the Gospel of John, however, shows that this is a very different kind of work. John presumes the existence of other gospels and takes a small number of scenes from Jesus' life and draws out their significance in lengthy and poetic meditations.

So the task of this little group, in a cramped bachelor flat, brought together by the light of a small candle around these ancient and sacred gospels, is no small work.

Their intention is to break open this story in a prayerful and honest manner so that they may better prepare themselves to more fully appreciate the Gospel when it is read at the Sunday Eucharist they will attend on the coming weekend.

"To really know a thing," Melbourne author Helen Garner says, "is to know it over and over again with the same new shock of discovery." The gospels often carry that same sense of discovery.

The belief of our ancient Church is that, little by little, the Gospel within the Mass works on our believing imagination, often in secret, in order to soften our hearts and slowly, over time, fashion and form us into a people worthy to be called Christian.

> *We are made of stories;*
> *we swap stories all day long;*
> *our religions are based on story;*
> *our education contains*
> *skeins of stories;*
> *our memories are constructed*
> *on stories.*
>
> ✳ ✳ ✳
>
> Brian Doyle, *Leaping revelations and epiphanies*,
> Loyola Press, Chicago, 2003

Did You Know

The gospels

- The word *Gospel* means 'Good News': the Good News that God has come to dwell among us and to invite us to a new kind of life. In a sense the Good News is Jesus.

- Some years after Jesus' Death and Resurrection, four different authors collected the stories and events of Jesus' life and wrote them down, describing them as 'the Good News'.

- Tradition gives us the names of these authors as Matthew, Mark, Luke and John.

- Today's scholars, however, are not absolutely sure who the writers were. Some speculate that the gospels were written and revised many times before the Church accepted them in their present form.

- Tradition believes that Matthew, the former tax collector and disciple of Jesus, wrote the gospel bearing his name. It is clear that this gospel was written for Jewish Christians profoundly shaken by the destruction of Jerusalem in the year 70. It may have been written first in Aramaic and later translated into Greek.

- It is believed that Mark was a member of the early church, perhaps even a secretary of St Peter, and wrote for a non-Jewish audience. Most scholars think this gospel was the first to be committed to writing and may have been used by Matthew and Luke as a source for their works.

- Luke never knew Jesus and is believed to be a physician and companion of St Paul. He wrote two books – the gospel that bears his name and The Acts of the Apostles. His gospel emphasises Jesus' concern for the poor and the powerless.

- The fourth gospel speaks of the 'beloved disciple'. Most think this is the apostle John, who is believed to have lived until almost the year 100 on the island of Patmos near present-day Turkey. This gospel was written some years after the first three gospels.

"What does it mean…?"

At one of the Easter parish masses, a proud grandfather brought his seven-year-old grandson to church. Apparently his parents didn't take him to church often, so he had a lot of whispered questions for his grandfather.

"Grand-dad, what happens when they pass the basket along?"

"That means they're giving their donations as gifts to the Lord," says the grandfather.

"What does it mean when the people bring in the bread and wine?"

"Well, the priest, Father Doherty, will take the gifts of the people, and they'll become the body and blood of Christ."

"And what does it mean when the priest touches his forehead, and his lips and his chest?"

"He is making a small cross on his head so that his mind will receive the message of the Gospel; his lips, so that his words will be true to the Gospel; and his heart, so that he will be touched by the Gospel," says the grandfather.

And the boy whispers, "What does it mean when Father Doherty takes his watch off and puts it on the pulpit?"

"Absolutely nothing, son," says the grandfather, "Absolutely nothing."

Listening to the Gospel 25

THE CREED
Our common struggle to believe

The tiny weatherboard church stood in the middle of sheep country – now caught in the steely talons of a ten-year drought. Another relentless sunset coloured the sky, as a small group of locals gathered to celebrate Easter – the Easter Vigil, in fact. (The colourful ceremony celebrated on the Saturday night before Easter Sunday). It was the third week of the month and the turn for their little parish to have the priest visit.

A couple in their late forties, Adrian and Rosemary, joined the group around the Easter fire. The Paschal candle was lit and led them into the shadowy church – the holy water stood gleaming in a glass bowl, as the celebrant began his renewal of baptismal promises…*Do you believe in one God?*

Rosemary caught her breath, struck by the impact of the simple question. *Do I believe?* she asked herself, as though facing the question for the first time in her life. *Really believe!* The memories flooded in. Their second son had died last year. Leukaemia. The bank was pressing for mortgage payments they didn't have. What remaining stock they had, standing forlorn in threadbare paddocks, were not worth the cost of transport to the market. She could hardly remember even the scent of rain. *Do you believe?* Her faith was paper-thin, her life rock-hard.

She believed in Adrian, her husband – weather-worn, laconic, didn't talk much, but a steady, reliable mate. She believed in her children – they were life itself. She believed in the land, even though it was a hard and unpredictable taskmaster.

Turning up to this tiny church once a month provided some anchor in an otherwise wave-swept sea. At its best, religion offers more than a list of answers designed to resolve the unanswerable. It offers a way to deal with the questions that plague our lives and puzzle our hearts. The best beliefs are those that have been tried and found to be consistent with the instincts of the rest of humankind over countless generations. Simple convictions such as:

There is something beyond us; there is something bigger than we are that calls on us; there is a purpose in life.

These beliefs have been tested and found to be true, not verified by science perhaps, but rise from somewhere deep in the human DNA. They may come as a spiritual insight erupting out of the struggles of humankind and jealously owned by generations of believers like a treasure hidden in a field. For the Christian believer, this belief is captured and given shape and colour in the extraordinary Good News brought to us by Jesus.

The same question, which challenges Rosemary, touches many of us who dare to explore below the surface of ritual and conventional belief. Not one of us can escape the bombardment of the secular and scientific discoveries that are the headlines of the nightly news. We live in a world exploding with

*I remember how, as a child,
when I contemplated
the sun, the moon, the stars,
and all the beautiful things
of nature,
I was wondering,
'who is the master of it all?'
And I felt a keen desire
to see Him,
to know Him
and to pay Him homage.*

Spe Salvi, #5, Encyclical Letter of Pope Benedict XVI,
November 2007

information, inundated with questions and clogged with moral dilemmas. How do we deal emotionally with a world split between starving millions on the one hand and packed supermarket shelves on the other; a planet that suffers Hurricane Katrina-like cyclones and rising sea levels; or the technological miracles of medicine that question the source of life itself and, at the same time, challenge its ethical limits?

And the casualties of belief are many. Nobel-prize-winning Irish poet Seamus Heaney reflects on his own life and the meaning and practice of his faith. He was born and raised a Catholic but for many years the practices and vocabulary of his early life slipped from him. Thirty years on, he chooses not to embrace entirely the faith of his adolescence, yet he is forced to admit a renewed appreciation of that spiritual undercurrent and a new sense of the sacred pervading his work.

The language of his Catholic past has found new power for him. In the poem "Out of this world" he catches depths in himself:

> *And yet I cannot disavow words like 'thanksgiving' and 'host' or 'communion bread'. They have an undying tremor and draw, like well water far down.*

> *You have made us for yourself, O God, and our heart is restless until it rests in you.*
>
> ✸ ✸ ✸
>
> St Augustine

The fading power of Catholic ritual and prayer, alas, is not uncommon in the lives of many who style themselves 'born Catholics', a term suggesting they have left those childish ideas far behind them. In the United States of America, for instance, statistics suggest that the largest religious denomination is Roman Catholic. The second largest – former Catholics. But many of these once-upon-a-time Catholics still recognise Heaney's "tremor and draw" – a deep-seated longing catches them with a certain surprise, as it were from the bottom of the well of their memories and dreams.

When we are challenged to say, as Rosemary was, *Do you believe in one God?*, it may be important to understand clearly what our faith teaches.

Belief is not contrary to science. To believe something is to know its truth not so much in our minds but in the centre of our souls. We believe in goodness, for instance, because however effective evil may seem to be, it contradicts the highest aspirations of our humanity. We believe in love, rather than hate, because love draws out the best in us, while hate feeds our pettiness.

The passenger jet flew 20,000 metres above the ocean.

Suddenly the Captain illuminated the seatbelt sign. "Would all passengers kindly resume their seats and fasten their seatbelts. We have struck some unexpected disturbance. All crew are to take their seats and discontinue serving."

The packed plane jumped around in the air. The turbulence became exceptional. Passengers began to become agitated and a little white-knuckled.

The flight attendant realised she had a Jewish rabbi and a Catholic priest aboard and approached them to see whether they could bring the passengers a little reassurance and help stop them panicking. The two clerics glanced at one another, and without a word, rose from their seats, one going to the front of the plane, the other to the rear – *and they took up a collection!*

28 A Friendly Guide to the Mass

DID YOU KNOW

The creed

- The word 'creed' comes from a Latin word for 'I believe' – *credo*.

- In the Bible itself there are examples of early Christian statements of belief, such as in St Paul's first letter to the church in Corinth:

  > For us there is one God, the Father from whom are all things and for whom we exist, and one Lord Jesus Christ from whom are all things and through whom we exist. (1 Cor. 8:6)

- In the first two centuries statements of faith began to evolve into the formula we call the Apostles' Creed, so called because the early Church understood that these basic beliefs came from the times of the apostles.

- For three centuries after the Resurrection, believers quietly accepted that Jesus was both God and human.

- By the year 300, some writers and theologians tried to explain away the mystery and say that Jesus was a wonderful human being and very much like God, but nothing more (or others took an opposite stance and claimed he was not really a man but a God in human form).

- In 325 the Church bishops met in Nicaea, a little town in what is now Turkey, and agreed on a set of beliefs which we call the Nicene Creed, and which we still say together at Sunday Mass.

- In the long history of the Church, new creeds have emerged in the light of new questions: the Council of Nicaea's Creed in the fourth century; the Athanasian Creed in the sixth century; and, even more recently, Pope Paul VI's "Credo of the People of God" in 1968.

We believe in the people whose hearts we hold in our hands, because we ourselves are nourished by that same relationship. We believe in the spirit within us because the material world simply contains not enough to reach "that well water deep down". We believe in God, not despite our restlessness, but because of it. As Augustine says, "You have made us for yourself, O God, and our heart is restless until it rests in you."

To say "I believe in God" means that I commit myself to make God a presence in the centre of my heart, in the humdrum of my days, in the sweat and blood of my struggles, and in the wonder and awe at the sight of a newly born baby. Discovering the way God works in each of these levels of my existence is the spiritual journey of a lifetime. At the celebration of each Sunday Mass, we – as a community of faith – are challenged to renew this belief in a God who resides deep down within the swirling mystery of life itself.

There are many names for God

Over the ages believers have employed many images and names for God. These are some of them.

God is a creative spirit, creator of all things. (Genesis 1:1)

God is a mother eagle teaching her young to fly. (Deuteronomy 32:11)

God is one who takes care of a difficult child. (Hosea 11:3)

God is a mother who is giving birth. (Isaiah 42)

God is one who prepares food and drink. (Isaiah 25:6)

God is a mother of a child. (Isaiah 49:15)

God is a midwife. (Isaiah 66:9)

God is one who washes and cleans. (Ezekiel 36:25)

God is one who washes away tears. (Isaiah 25:8)

God is Abba (the Jewish word for 'daddy' in Mark 14:36)

God is a grower of vines. (John 15:1)

God the Father and I are one. (Jesus, speaking of his Father in John 10:30)

The language people have employed to describe this 'gracious mystery' has taken many forms.

God is a Trinity, Father, Son and Holy Spirit. (Council of Nicea in 325)

God in whom we live and move and have our being. (Acts of the Apostles 17:28)

God is the source and destiny of all.

God is the ground of all being.

God is a loving and consoling friend who helps us without fail.

God is the guarantor of ultimate meaning or the ultimate meaning itself.

God is a male spirit in the sky who sees, knows and influences all. (This is a popular but seriously limited image.)

A short history of the Mass

During the lifetime of Jesus of Nazareth

Jesus would have learned to pray as he ate with his family at home.

For a pious Jew every meal was a sacred act.

A meal and its blessing recalled God's faithful generosity.

A meal was a reminder of the ancient and faithful covenant with God.

A pious Jew would bless God when breaking bread, seeing lightning, purchasing something, watching a sunset as well as other significant moments in life.

A pious Jew would pray in the temple, in the synagogue and at home.

As an adult, Jesus' table ministry was both an act of hospitality and an act of unconditional acceptance.

After the Resurrection of Jesus Christ

The early Christian community would gather for 'the breaking of the bread'.

Believers would gather in people's homes as well as in borrowed rooms in public buildings. The Good News was announced, teaching was imparted and reconciliation was offered.

It was not uncommon to find spacious homes of wealthy believers with large dining rooms and a pool in an atrium suitable for baptism.

These gatherings would normally have included a meal with the Eucharist.

Emerging Christianity (100–313)

At first Christianity appeared as a movement within Judaism, rather than as a religion distinct from it.

It was not long before Christianity spread to the non-Jewish world and was recognised as 'catholic' – that is, all-embracing, open to all nations and peoples of various religious backgrounds.

Christians observed Sunday (the day of the Resurrection, the beginning of the 'new creation') as the primary day for public worship.

Jewish Christians, of course, continued to celebrate the Sabbath.

By the end of the first century Christianity grew to almost twenty thousand followers and, by the year 300, it grew to five to seven million in a Roman Empire of fifty or sixty million.

Conflict with the Roman authorities grew, often erupting in persecution.

From Nero in the year 64 to Diocletian in the year 303 the authorities found reasons to persecute Christian groups – though sporadic over this time and often confined to specific geographical areas, the persecutions were separated by long periods of peace.

Christian groups followed a variety of approaches to the Eucharist, but there exists one early and valuable description from an open letter to the Emperor written by the Christian philosopher, Justin Martyr. (See page 12.)

the voice of the worshippers, especially in places where Latin was not the language of normal believers.

Much of the worship was sung rather than spoken – there was little public speech that was not musical to some degree.

The best known body of Latin musical chant was known as Gregorian chant, which arose after a long and complex history.

During this period, the "Sanctus" ("Holy, Holy, Holy") about the fourth century, the "Gloria" ("Glory be to God") about the late fourth century and the "Agnus Dei" ("Lamb of God") about the seventh century gradually became part of the prayers of the Mass.

In this period there was a movement from more improvised prayer in the Mass to more standardised liturgical texts with Latin as their language.

Rome becomes the centre of Christianity (313–750)

The Emperor Constantine recognised the right of all religions to exist (in "The Edict of Milan"), and his support of the Christian faith led to a process of Christianisation that would sweep through the empire. From being regarded as an illegal sect, Christianity was transformed into the preferred religion of the empire.

Impressive buildings for Christian worship were constructed.

Bishops were granted various honours and wore the insignia of civil magistrates.

During a time when the dominant language was Greek, Latin emerged as the language of Christian worship and theology.

Every book of the New Testament had been written in Greek. The turn to Latin would have a clear and lasting effect on Christian life and practice.

In worship there was a gradual diminishment of

The Middle Ages (750–1070)

There was an architectural renaissance during this period.

Churches in this era were shaped to respect the increased separation between clergy and laity.

Bells became of increasing importance.

Christians crisscrossed Europe on pilgrimage.

In earlier times the altar was a wooden table, often moveable, usually placed in the body of the church so that the community could gather around three sides of it; the celebrant stood on whatever side that allowed him to face East, the place of the rising sun and symbol of the Resurrection.

Over time the altar was pushed further towards the back of the church until it ended up close to or against the back wall, with the celebrant facing the altar and his back to the people.

Stone altars now became the norm.

Relics of saints were deposited in the altar as part of the ritual of consecration of a church.

The celebration of daily Mass became common.

The development of an area for the choir (men and boys) was common; lay people were restricted from designated areas close to the altar.

Screens were sometimes built to separate the choir and altar from the main part of the cathedral.

The High Middle Ages (1000–1500)

This was the time of the Crusades and of exploration of the world outside Europe.

There was a reassertion of papal influence and control of the church.

Roman direction of liturgical practice and the Eucharist not seen before was notable.

The 'Breviary' was developed – the obligation of clerics to pray the 'Prayer of the church' was abridged into an abbreviated and more manageable form.

The rise of the great universities, such as Paris, Bologna and Oxford, occurred during this period.

The rise of charismatic lay preachers, such as Francis of Assisi, occurred at this time.

The High Middle Ages was one of the most inventive periods in the history of church architecture.

This era saw the development of two significant architectural styles for cathedrals – Gothic and Italian Renaissance.

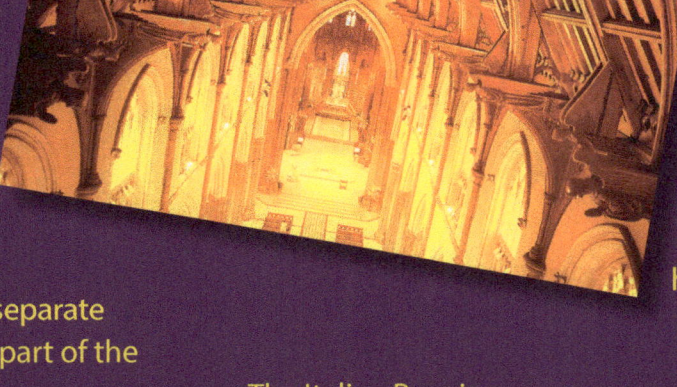

Gothic architecture embodied particular views of what it meant to be a church; every ministry and person had an assigned place and role in a well-defined hierarchical order.

The Italian Renaissance, a powerful new social and artistic movement, emphasised the value, dignity and unity of human nature.

Private Masses became popular.

There was increased veneration of the relics of saints.

The popes leave Rome for Avignon in France from 1309 to 1377.

Elevation of the host at the Eucharistic Prayer became common; only much later was the chalice elevated.

The emphasis in the celebration of Mass became what the congregation could see, rather than on what they could hear.

The Reformation and Counter-Reformation (1500–1900)

Saint Peter's in Rome was under reconstruction.

This was a time of ecclesiastical upheaval and radical reshaping of Western Christianity.

The reforming ideas of Martin Luther rejected much of the traditional understanding of the Eucharist.

In response to this upheaval, the Council of Trent (1545–63) brought a new uniformity in both the doctrine and rubric of the Mass.

In the face of challenges to the traditional understanding of the Eucharist mounted by the reformers – notably Luther, Calvin and Zwingli – the Council of Trent proclaimed that Christ was 'truly, really and substantially contained' in the Eucharist, which was consistently referred to as the 'Sacrifice of the Mass'.

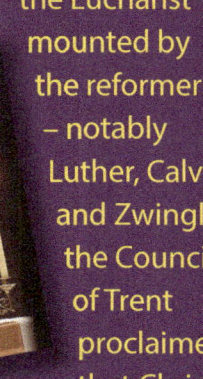

Certain standards of architectural design and furnishings became common.

Where previously the Eucharist was reserved in a vessel suspended above the altar (or elsewhere), now the placing of the reserved Eucharist in a tabernacle fixed on the altar became common.

Confessionals became a part of church design.

Holy water fonts were placed in church entrances.

Fixed pews took the place of moveable and more flexible seating.

The twentieth century

In 1900 there were 1.6 billion people on the planet; in 2000, over 6 billion.

During the twentieth century 200 million lives were lost in violence and war.

The development of philosophy and political theory moved towards a clearer understanding of the dignity of the individual.

Movements of human liberation called for greater inclusion and equality across the divides of gender, ethnicity, social class and age.

From the time of Pope Pius X the church called for more active participation among lay people at the Mass.

Experiments with the use of the local language (rather than Latin) were made in places such as Yugoslavia as early as 1929.

'Dialogue Masses', in which the priest and the congregation would engage in a series of statements and responses, were being used as early as 1939.

Pope Pius XII published *Mediator Dei* in 1947, in which lay worshippers were called to a more active participation at Mass in contrast to their former passive role.

The Second Vatican Council (1962–65) produced a pivotal document entitled the *Constitution of the Sacred Liturgy* in the reform of how the Mass and many of the sacraments were to be celebrated. A stronger emphasis was placed on 'active participation of the congregation' and the Mass was celebrated in the vernacular.

THE PRAYERS OF THE FAITHFUL
The General Intercessions

One of the oldest parts of the Mass is the General Intercessions, popularly called the Prayers of the Faithful. These prayers are a continuation of certain ritual practices of the Jewish Synagogue which were a series of blessings containing requests for individual people and also for the needs of the world.

For a moment let us reflect on this ancient word 'prayer'.

Prayer is one of life's mysteries. Its roots in the deep history of humankind are quite uncertain. We really know nothing of it origins. Where did it come from? How did humankind find itself praying? We don't know. It is in all the holy books and has its own expression in all the variety of the world's religions. In the books of the Bible, prayer is simply a matter of course. To begin with Israel had no word for 'pray'. The word for 'praying' contained within its meaning the concept of rejoicing, laughing, crying, reviling and imploring according to how one felt. Glance at any example from the ancient book of Psalms and you will catch an idea of how these people prayed.

The entire Mass is, of course, a prayer. The General Intercessions, however, provides an opportunity to direct that prayer. We are invited to pray for others.

Praying for other people makes us keenly aware of them. To recognise their part in our life expresses our desire to be bound to them in love, wanting to support them and even, at times, to bear their burdens.

Such prayers are a powerful exercise of memory and a desire to be awake to what is happening in our own set of relationships. We look around us in our own world today and listen to its voices, in danger of becoming lost in its vastness and yet in the act of prayer we take an opportunity of recognising the critical issues which sometimes challenge the very community in which we live.

Engaging in these prayers we dig deep and proclaim our existence as human beings, recognising the responsibilities we share in being citizens of a fragile planet and members of a struggling pilgrim people of God.

The General Intercessions are prayed after we have heard the reading from scripture (and the homily, in which the celebrant reflects on aspects of the readings that touch our lives). They are our response to the many challenges which the Word of God places before us. The celebrant calls those gathered to take time in prayer, reminding people perhaps of the season of the year (Advent or Lent, for example) and the particular reason for this celebration (a funeral, a marriage or a parish event). A member of the congregation (or perhaps a deacon) then recites a series of prayer intentions to which the congregation responds. The celebrant then allows time for each person to search their heart in silent prayer, which at times in certain celebrations may lead an individual to share their prayer aloud with the rest of the congregation.

There is a certain sequence in the petitions. The first prayer is normally for the needs of the Church. Then follows a prayer for leadership in our communities and public life, including the pressing issues of the day. The third category of prayer is for people who are oppressed or marginalised in any way. The fourth category directs its attention to the issues facing the local community of faith. Time is then provided for silent prayer of the gathered people, before the celebrant asks God to accept these prayers on behalf of this community.

Prayer has been described as an act of faith in which The General Intercessions at Mass are an action of what is called our 'baptismal priesthood'. It can be described as a priestly act "to pray for this bruised world in which we live".

The prayers of the faithful 35

The Liturgy of the Eucharist

Preparing the Bread and the Wine
Are these gifts as simple as they seem?

A striking photograph was hanging on the wall of the church vestibule.

A simple inscription read, 'Earth Rise'. It famously depicts the view of planet earth apparently rising out of the rim of the moon. Taken almost by accident by astronaut Frank Borman, it is ranked by some as one of the most significant photographs of our time. It is an image, so powerful and eloquent, that it still retains a freshness that can take your breath away forty years later. Borman has captured, almost without realising it, humanity's first glimpse of this exquisite, blue-green planet taken from the far side of the moon – a breathlessly beautiful, but quite tiny globe set against the darkness and immensity of space – finite, vulnerable and, from that distant perspective, a common home which offers life and meaning to its six billion human inhabitants.

But what is this photo doing in the church vestibule? And what significance does it hold for people gathering to engage in their weekly act of worship?

The first part of the Mass concludes with the statement of faith in the creed followed by our collective prayer (the Prayers of the Faithful). The mood changes when the gifts of bread and wine are carried to the altar in the part of the ceremony called 'the Offertory'. In this part of the Mass, the celebrant receives these gifts, places them on the altar and prepares for the main Prayer of the Eucharist.

There are many parts of the Mass that are more important than the Offertory of the Mass. However, the wider significance of these unspectacular gifts of 'ordinary' bread and 'ordinary' wine and what they are meant to represent can sometimes be underestimated.

"It is the gift of all poets," Margery Sharp observes, "to find depth in the commonplace." And the Offertory of the Mass challenges the poet in us to recognise the layer upon layer of meaning they represent.

The small wafer of bread and the flask of wine carry the weight of centuries of significance. Their simplicity stirs the imagination to capture the depths of what they represent and what they become in the mystery of the Mass.

When the celebrant lifts up the bread ("which earth has given and human hands have made"), there is so much more than a small wafer being offered to God, the creator of all things. These apparently modest gifts brought from the midst of the gathered congregation serve to represent the entire panoply of what has been given to us in the very act of creation. Lifting up the cup of wine, with the words "fruit of the vine and work of human hands", the priest reminds us that this offering stands for all of the abundance of life that have been given to us in the continuing act of creation – every living thing, every created thing, every product of human ingenuity, all music

*We can free our life and the world
from the poisons and contaminations
that could destroy the present and the future.
We can uncover the sources of creation
and keep them unsullied,
and in this way we can make a right use of creation,
which comes to us as a gift,
according to its intrinsic requirements
and ultimate purpose.
This makes sense even if outwardly we achieve nothing
or seem powerless in the face of
overwhelming hostile forces.
So on the one hand,
our actions engender hope for us and for others;
but at the same time, it is the great hope
based upon God's promises
that gives us courage and directs our action
in good times and bad.*

Spe Salvi, Encyclical Letter of Pope Benedict XVI, November 2007

and art of any kind, in fact, the entire cornucopia of this fragile blue-green planet. Later, this will be made crystal clear in the Prayer of the Eucharist: "All creation rightly gives you praise".

So during this preparation of gifts, it is scarcely possible to ignore how badly we have treated this planet – the place given to us by our generous God in words some would describe as 'the primary sacrament' of life. These simple gifts of bread and wine remind us of the damage we human beings are doing to the earth from which they have been made. We have damaged the atmosphere, the soil, the rivers and the seas of this planet. These simple items of bread and wine serve as a reminder of the violence, hunger and lack of education in which so many children and families pursue their life goals.

These prayers contain an echo of the ancient Jewish prayer forms used in the synagogues and especially in their homes, and, above all, in the Passover meal – these prayers all begin with a blessing of the gifts of creation, a creation captured as perhaps never before by the photograph taken from the far side of the moon all those years ago.

This historic photo, 'Earth Rise', described by nature photographer Galen Powell as "the most influential environmental photograph ever taken" stands as an eloquent illustration not only of a deeper appreciation of the Earth's beauty, and that it is our shared home, but also that the Earth is connected to the simple act of lifting bread and wine in our prayer at this part of the Mass. It reminds us that this home of ours is irreplaceable and delivers the stark message of the grave responsibility we all share for the care of this fragile world.

"In the Eucharist" Australian theologian Denis Edwards remarks, "the Christian community naturally focuses on Christ's liberating death and resurrection, but what is often forgotten is that every Eucharist is a thanksgiving memorial for God at work in creation as well as the redemption."

The central prayer of the Eucharist
Promising to live as sacred people

A young boy became seriously ill and was diagnosed with a life-threatening blood disease. A search went out for a compatible blood donor but none could be found. Then it was discovered that his six-year-old sister shared his blood type. The mother and father sat down with her to ask if she would be willing to donate blood to save the life of her brother. To their surprise, she didn't answer right away. She needed some time to think about it. After a few days she came back to her mother and announced that she would do it.

The following day the doctor brought both children to his clinic and placed them on cots next to each other. He wanted to let them see how one was helping the other. First he drew a half pint of blood from the young girl's arm. Then he moved it over to her brother's cot and inserted the needle so his sister could see the effect. In a few minutes colour began to pour back into his cheeks.

Then the girl motioned to the doctor to come over. She wanted to ask a question. Very quietly, she whispered, "Will I start to die right away?"

The story of the Last Supper is the story of a young man dying for what he believed. The prayer at the centre of the Eucharist recalls the actions and significance of this sacred meal. Collectively, we remember how on the night before he was killed, Jesus took bread and wine and declared these to be his body and blood. This was to be a night of long shadows. He was to be betrayed by Judas and denied by Peter, and during the next day most of his other young friends would hide themselves in fright when the soldiers came to arrest him.

The little sister's quiet question threw light on her unobtrusive courage, as she misunderstood the gift she was being asked to share with her brother. She believed she was being asked to trade her life for her brother's. No wonder she needed a day or two to mull it over.

The words of Jesus allow none of this misunderstanding. In the words of the Mass during the Eucharistic Prayer, the celebrant firstly takes bread and then the cup of wine while saying:

Take this, all of you, and eat of it:
for this is my Body which will be given up for you.

Take this, all of you, and drink from it:
for this is the chalice of my Blood,
the Blood of the new and eternal covenant.

With all of the value of hindsight, the Christian community reads these words as a prelude to the act of love Jesus carries out the next day on the hill of Calvary. Generations of believers have faithfully followed the invitation to continue this meal – *in memory of me*.

But what is the implication of our taking this body and blood? Perhaps there is a clue to the answer in the words "the new and everlasting covenant".

'Covenant' is an ancient Jewish concept which is understood as a sacred agreement between the God of Israel and the people of Israel. It was a self-understanding consecrated through the years of their turbulent history and their leaders, Abraham, Moses and the prophets. They believed they were 'the chosen people' –'I will be your God and you will be my people'.

Did You Know

The Consecration of the bread and the wine

- Jesus Christ came into the world to bring all humankind back to the Father.

- At Mass, the culminating moment comes at what we call 'the consecration'. At this central action of the Mass, the priest uses the very words and gestures of Jesus at the Last Supper. The priest acts *in persona Christi*, that is, in the person of Christ.

- This part of the Eucharistic Prayer is called the 'institutional narrative' because it follows carefully the words of the gospel describing what Jesus did at the Last Supper and asks those who would follow him 'to do this in memory of me' (Lk 22:19).

- His actions are direct; his words are simple and straightforward. Taking the bread, the celebrant holds it before him, bows slightly and repeats the words of Jesus from long ago:

   Take this, all of you, and eat of it:
   for this is my Body which will be given up for you.

- The bread and wine are consecrated separately, because this is what Jesus did with his young friends.

   Take this, all of you, and drink from it:
   for this is the chalice of my Blood,
   the Blood of the new and eternal covenant
   which will be poured out for you
   and for many for the forgiveness of sins.
   Do this in memory of me.

- The church teaches that Jesus, the Risen Christ, is truly present in both the bread and the chalice.

- The Risen Christ is now present on the altar. The celebrant genuflects reverently to acknowledge this astonishing reality.

- Jesus gives himself totally to us, which is dramatised by his hands outstretched on the cross in our faith's greatest act of love and friendship.

When we come to celebrate Mass, we are identifying ourselves as the 'people of the new and everlasting covenant' – a covenant sealed by Jesus' gift of himself to his Father and to us, on Calvary. As a result, when we receive the body and blood of Christ in communion, it is not only an act of faith, but a serious act of commitment which contains a promise to live as a sacred people. The faith we celebrate in the Eucharist is not simply a matter of believing certain teachings about God. Faith is itself a 'covenant' – that is, becoming conscious of a relationship that already exists because the Father of Jesus has been in relationship with us from the beginning, whether we believe it or not. Christian faith is not about believing but about faithfulness – fidelity to that relationship.

In the Mass, we are drawn into this ancient ritual meal understanding three key beliefs: first, that it is the Risen Lord who nourishes us with this bread and wine; second, Christ makes us one with himself; and, lastly, that he makes us one with each other. In the Gospel of John, it is stated that "he who eats my flesh and drinks my blood has eternal life" (John 6:54) and "he who eats my flesh and drinks my blood abides in me and I in him" (John 6:56).

The Prayer of the Eucharist is a prayer of courage and love. As the little sister decided to offer her life's blood to enable her brother to live, so Jesus of Nazareth offers his life for those he loves. Our sharing the Risen Christ in communion binds us together as a loving community committed to bring that love to our bruised and broken world, and to act with all of the necessary courage that such action will require. Such love is not mere poetry.

In the course of World War I, the story was told of a young sergeant who begged his commanding officer to allow him to go back onto the battlefield to rescue his fallen friend. "If you do that, we'll lose you both," the officer said. But the sergeant begged and the officer relented.

After the battle, when the battalion was finally able to retrieve both bodies, the sergeant, seriously wounded, was still alive but deteriorating rapidly.

"Now do you see how useless it was to go out there?" the officer demanded.

"Oh, no, sir, it was all worth it. You see, when I finally got to him, he said to me, 'Jack, I knew you'd come,'" the sergeant whispered as he breathed his last breath.

Real love often requires real courage. Genuine love does not count the cost.

Eucharistic Prayers

In 1968 the church developed a number of Eucharistic Prayers to add to the so-called 'Roman Canon', which had been the only formulation for years before that time.

Firstly, the Roman Canon was slightly modified (now known as Eucharistic Prayer 1), and then three other formulations were published known as Eucharistic Prayer 2, Eucharistic Prayer 3 and Eucharistic Prayer 4.

In 1974 three Eucharistic Prayers for children were approved; and also two Eucharistic Prayers for reconciliation to be used when reconciliation is the central matter of concern.

Eucharistic Prayer 1 (known as the Roman Canon) goes back to the fourth century, undergoing certain elaborations in the sixth century under Pope Gregory the Great. By the second half of the ninth century it came to be prayed in a low voice, probably to emphasise the notion of 'mystery'. It was only in the 1960s that the presiding celebrant was encouraged to say this prayer aloud.

Eucharistic Prayer 2, extremely brief and simple, is based on a model which dates back to the early third century and is usually attributed to Hippolytus of Rome.

Eucharistic Prayer 3 incorporates the general themes of the Roman Canon and enriches them with formulas from other liturgical traditions.

Eucharistic Prayer 4 draws much of its formulation from Eastern sources and, following their example, continues the theme of praise throughout the prayer.

The Eucharistic Prayers for children are characterised by the use of acclamations throughout the prayer.

A COMMUNITY GATHERED HERE

She liked sitting in *that* seat – three from the back and right at the end of the pew. Something about having your own emotional space away from the crowd. With the reliability of a Swiss railway timetable, she always arrived three minutes early, perhaps just to secure her place. (We all have our harmless rituals, it seems, which have little to do with the ancient rite of the Mass.)

At the tinkling of the bell, which announced that the sacred host would be elevated, she would lift her head, perhaps for the first time and engage with the liturgical moment. It seemed all so distant from that night in the upper room with his disciples.

At the Last Supper, when Jesus said, "This is my body", he probably wasn't simply talking about the bread in his hands. He was talking about the community gathered there. About their love and care, about their being together again. He was talking about himself, Christ present as teacher, healer, leader. He was talking about sharing a meal in solidarity. He was talking about all the sharing they had done over the years. He was talking, in short, about his body, the body of Christ, which Paul would write about so elegantly later in his letters. The bread taken at the Last Supper, is not to be separated from the community, not to be taken away from the people gathered there.

To what extent is this appreciated by the quiet soul in the shadowy corner in the back of the church?

This sacrificial meal is not just bread and wine turned into the body and blood of Christ – no matter how explosively true such a belief is. It is bread *broken* and wine *poured out*. It is a person's life broken for others and a person's blood poured out for this community of faith.

Many Catholics, perhaps like our shy worshipper, limit their understanding to what happens at Mass as being intensely personal – *it is between Jesus and me*. The notion of a shared moment with other believers – a holy moment of unity, a sacrament which links our concerns with everyone here and with all those we know and love, and indeed with the issues of the wider community – is often overlooked.

The body of Christ for Jesus and his early followers, such as Paul, was clearly the community brought together by the Risen Christ. Each time a reference is made to the body and its parts, it is a reference to the people.

To appreciate what is happening at Mass, particularly at the Eucharistic Prayer, those present need to have a profound acceptance of the community both gathered and absent. The Eucharist challenges us to a renewed reverence of the body of Christ – for the outsiders, those on the streets, those excluded because of our narrow norms, for the dirty and the hungry, for children in poverty, for the wealthy locked in a paralysis of spirit.

When the priest says "The body of Christ" in the communion service, he is saying, "Do you accept the community here – these people with their weaknesses, their petty vanities, their boring habits, their annoying differences?" The answer is "Yes I do accept this responsibility of living in the body of Christ. Yes, these are my sisters and brothers and so are those others in the turbulent world outside these walls – all of them. Amen."

It is the Risen Jesus' gift of himself in communion that enables us to recognise the "body of Christ" and what we can be and do as the body of Christ: give our lives in love to God and to our sisters and brothers.

When the Gospel of John comes to give an account of what happened at the Last Supper, curiously the evangelist does not mention Jesus taking bread and wine. At the end of the evening, as John describes the scene, Jesus gets up from table and spends time with each person there, washing their feet in a most intimate fashion. Here was his expression of personal care and love, so profound, that we can scarcely imagine it. This was a dramatic moment of healing and reconciliation, and an unmistakable challenge to those young friends to minister to people in the same fashion wherever they would find them in the future. This is, for John and for us as well, the moment when the body of Christ is embraced, cared for, and recognised. The Eucharist is a sacrament of the heart as well as the body.

And then there is us – we who come to celebrate hoping for some sort of a breakthrough this week; most of us being not terribly evil or incredibly good. We – who are scattered through the church, locked into our own concerns, distracted by our own limitations – hear the words "This is the body of Christ" and are challenged to recognise our new identity. "We are the body of Christ" gathered here and across this planet. Our ministry is to make peace, establish justice and recognise the immense potential we carry to bring some sense of reconciliation to a broken world, according to the power and purpose of Jesus Christ within us.

This is the common challenge to everyone who shares this Eucharist. This is true no matter where we choose to sit in Church or in whichever way we attempt to guard our anonymity.

> *The origins of the Eucharistic Prayer are to be found in a series of table prayers required at every Jewish meal. Before eating the meal the father of the family uttered the Jewish prayer of blessing, known in Hebrew as the berakah, which praised God.*
>
> Jewish origins of the Eucharistic Prayer

DID YOU KNOW

The eight elements of the Eucharistic Prayer

- **The Prayer of Thanksgiving** – The word Eucharist means 'thanksgiving', so the entire prayer is governed by the notion of thanksgiving, which is given direction by the preface.

- **The Acclamation** – Every Mass includes three acclamations: the "Holy, Holy, Holy", the memorial acclamation such as "Christ has died, Christ is Risen, Christ will come again" and the "Great Amen" with which the congregation all acknowledge their commitment to the prayer.

- **The Petition** – Asking for the Holy Spirit to come down on the gifts. The formal Greek word for this is the *Epiclesis*.

- **The Institutional Narrative and Consecration** – The most solemn moment of the Mass takes place at this point. The words of the Last Supper are used to identify the bread and wine with Jesus' body and blood handed over for our own sake.

- **The Memorial of the Death, Resurrection and Ascension of the Lord** – We are a religion of 'memory'. The formal Greek word for this is *Anamnesis*.

- **The Offering** – The action of the offering of ourselves with Christ to the Father. "From the many gifts you have given us, we offer to you God of glory and majesty…" (Eucharistic Prayer 1)

- **The Intercessions** – The prayer that we be united in communion with one another "May we be filled with the Holy Spirit and become one body, one spirit in Christ" (Eucharistic Prayer 3); that we share the inheritance of the saints; that we pray for the Pope, the local bishop, the clergy and the whole Church as well as our local assembly. Finally, we show our solidarity and loving memory for those who have died.

- **The Final Doxology** – All the Eucharistic Prayers end as they began, with the praise and glory of God. They emphasise that Christ is the centre, the content and the energy of our prayer to which the congregation replies "Amen".

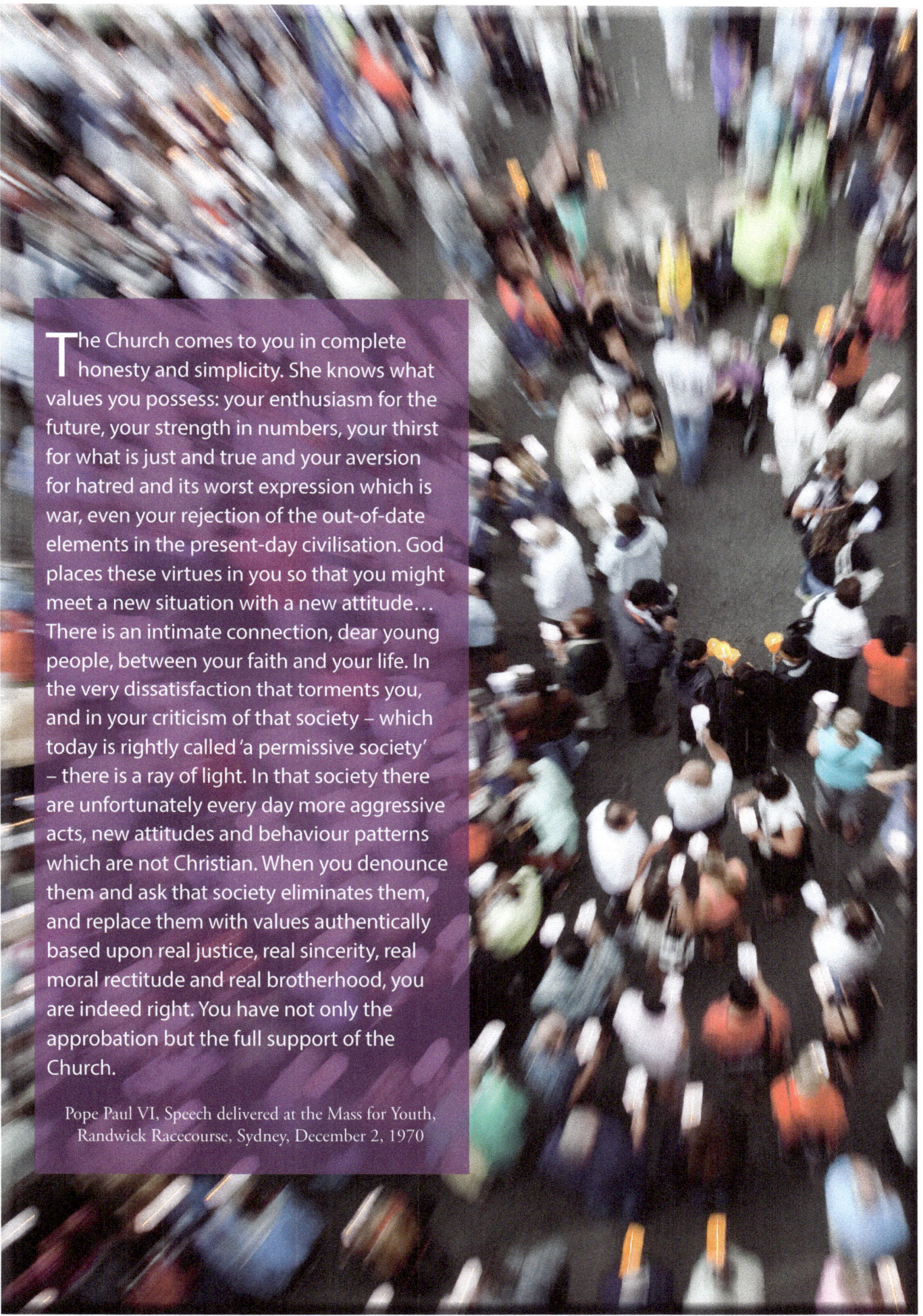

The Church comes to you in complete honesty and simplicity. She knows what values you possess: your enthusiasm for the future, your strength in numbers, your thirst for what is just and true and your aversion for hatred and its worst expression which is war, even your rejection of the out-of-date elements in the present-day civilisation. God places these virtues in you so that you might meet a new situation with a new attitude… There is an intimate connection, dear young people, between your faith and your life. In the very dissatisfaction that torments you, and in your criticism of that society – which today is rightly called 'a permissive society' – there is a ray of light. In that society there are unfortunately every day more aggressive acts, new attitudes and behaviour patterns which are not Christian. When you denounce them and ask that society eliminates them, and replace them with values authentically based upon real justice, real sincerity, real moral rectitude and real brotherhood, you are indeed right. You have not only the approbation but the full support of the Church.

Pope Paul VI, Speech delivered at the Mass for Youth, Randwick Racecourse, Sydney, December 2, 1970

THE SIGN OF PEACE
Recognising the sacred in others

The Mass is always calling us to peace, to reconciliation with one another and to a sense of justice that recognises the rights of others.

In some earlier times, this gesture of peace was placed somewhere between the scriptural readings and the beginning of the Eucharistic Prayer. The Roman rite (the rite we use), however, places this prayer and gesture of peace in close proximity to the time we receive Holy Communion. The intention is quite clear. We need to be reconciled and at peace with others in order to receive Holy Communion. The message is quite unambiguous – that being in communion with the Lord means being in communion with one another at the same time.

The "Pastoral Introduction to the Order of the Mass" proposed by the International Commission on English in the Liturgy gives one of the best interpretations of the sign of peace in its present location:

The exchange of peace prior to the reception of communion is an acknowledgment that Christ whom we receive in the sacrament is already present in our neighbour. In this exchange the assembly acknowledges the insistent Gospel truth that communion with God in Christ is enjoyed in communion with our sisters and brothers in Christ. The rite of peace is not an expression merely of human solidarity or good will; it is rather an opening of ourselves and our neighbours to a challenge and a gift from beyond ourselves. Like the Amen at communion, it is the acceptance of a challenge, a profession of faith that we are members, one with another, in the body of Christ.

In a planet riven with the ugly reality of war and mayhem, in cities marked with the brutality of crime and homelessness, in domestic situations of violence and grief, each time we celebrate the Eucharist we are challenged with the responsibility to be genuine bearers of peace.

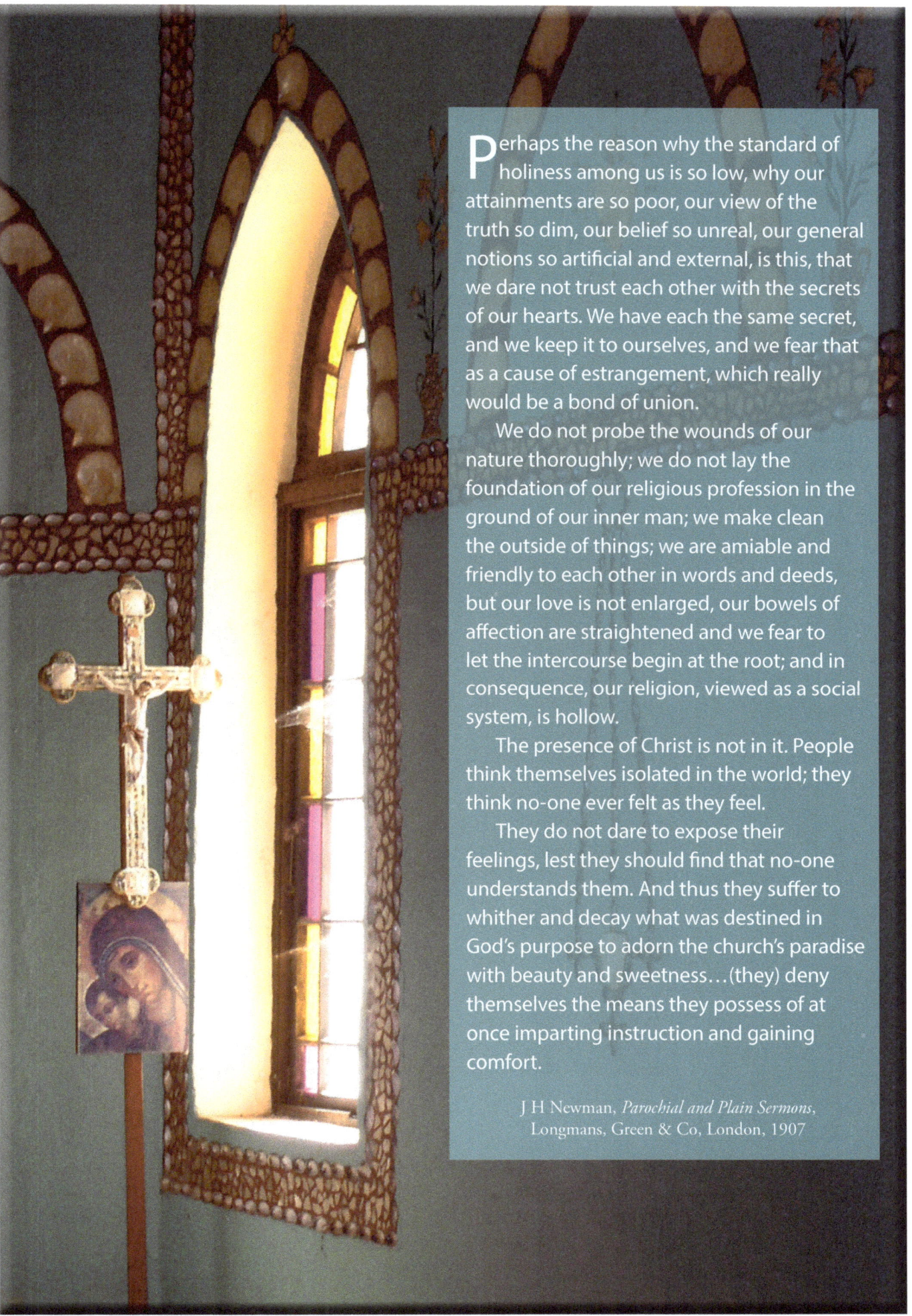

Perhaps the reason why the standard of holiness among us is so low, why our attainments are so poor, our view of the truth so dim, our belief so unreal, our general notions so artificial and external, is this, that we dare not trust each other with the secrets of our hearts. We have each the same secret, and we keep it to ourselves, and we fear that as a cause of estrangement, which really would be a bond of union.

We do not probe the wounds of our nature thoroughly; we do not lay the foundation of our religious profession in the ground of our inner man; we make clean the outside of things; we are amiable and friendly to each other in words and deeds, but our love is not enlarged, our bowels of affection are straightened and we fear to let the intercourse begin at the root; and in consequence, our religion, viewed as a social system, is hollow.

The presence of Christ is not in it. People think themselves isolated in the world; they think no-one ever felt as they feel.

They do not dare to expose their feelings, lest they should find that no-one understands them. And thus they suffer to whither and decay what was destined in God's purpose to adorn the church's paradise with beauty and sweetness…(they) deny themselves the means they possess of at once imparting instruction and gaining comfort.

J H Newman, *Parochial and Plain Sermons*, Longmans, Green & Co, London, 1907

Holy Communion
Unveiling the lion in the marble

There is a story about Michelangelo which says that when he worked with his sculpting chisel, he believed that he was simply revealing a hidden form already existing in the block of marble.

In his book *Clowning in Rome* the late Henri Nouwen tells a similar story:

> There once was a sculptor working hard with his hammer and chisel on a large block of marble. A little boy who was watching him saw nothing more than large and small pieces of stone falling away left and right. He had no idea what was happening. But when the boy returned to the studio a few weeks later, he saw, to his great surprise, a large powerful lion sitting in the place where the marble had stood. With great excitement the boy ran to the sculptor and said, "Sir, tell me, how did you know there was a lion in the marble?"

Most of us can expend great effort in searching for our true selves. This 'true self' is a thing of beauty existing in the marble of our daily existence – often masked by a 'false self', which keeps us captive in its counterfeit wiles. With great accuracy, writer Thomas Merton, whose literary genius awoke the spiritual needs of a generation of searchers, threw some light on the presence of this 'true self' within each person. Merton identified that the inner struggle each of us experiences is between what can be called our 'true self' and our 'false self'. This search for our true self, that part of us which is most authentic and honest, is one way of describing the universal quest we experience for meaning and happiness.

To share the Eucharist in communion with our fellow searchers is to cut through that superficiality and unreality of what we could call the 'false self' and risk sharing the sacred meal in memory of the one who died for what he believed. And as the Risen Christ is encountered in the reception of communion, we also embrace that risen life, recognising the real truth of who we are. When the Risen Christ appeared to his dispirited disciples locked in fear and dismay at their betrayal and abandonment of him at Calvary, his greeting was one word – *shalom*. "Peace I give you, my peace I leave with you." This is the gift the believer receives in Holy Communion.

Another way of understanding our true selves can be seen in the writing of Canadian novelist Jane Urquhart. As the daughter of a medical practitioner, she remembers playing with her father's stethoscope:

> I loved the rubber earpiece that shut out the noise of the world. But even more, I loved the little silver bell at the end of the double hose, a bell I could place against my chest in order to listen to the drum… the pounding music of my own complicated, fascinating heart.

At a deep level, at the level of our 'true self', we generally have a feeling that ultimately things make sense; that there is a moral underpinning to everything; that love has a meaning and that we are called to give ourselves to some higher good – this is the quiet voice that resides, undetected by the most sensitive stethoscope, deep within each "complicated, fascinating heart".

Our lives are always smaller than our dreams – in a sense, our lives are always too small for us.

To share the Eucharist and to receive communion at Mass expands our normal shrunken vision. There is more mystery within one ordinary, precious life than can be measured.

The powerful Jewish insight, which emerges from the first book of the Bible, and continues its beautiful melody throughout all of the scriptural story is that *we are made in the image and likeness of God*. We are fashioned in Love's image.

This is 'the true self' – that suffers the persistent battering of the consumerist culture, which beats on the corrugated iron roof of our life like a violent hailstorm.

God gives nothing to those who keep their arms crossed

That 'Love', so powerfully pictured in the book of Genesis, has fashioned the sun and the stars and the entire cosmos in general, and humanity in particular, and has come to *dwell among us*. We come into intimate touch with that gracious God in communion. We encounter this stunning truth each time we are offered "the body and blood of Christ". And yet, our fragile and frightened hearts make us so reluctant to even entertain the possibility of such a Love having anything to do with our mundane lives.

Receiving the Eucharist in Holy Communion, we open ourselves to recover this appreciation of who we really are. Our true self, often distorted and mangled by the competing claims of our society, is revealed, like the beautiful and majestic lion within the marble, as a creation made in the image and likeness of God.

"God gives nothing to those who keep their arms crossed," says an African proverb. To receive the Risen Christ in communion, we open our arms and stretch out our hands. We open ourselves to all those who receive the Eucharist with us, to all believers, and ultimately to all humankind.

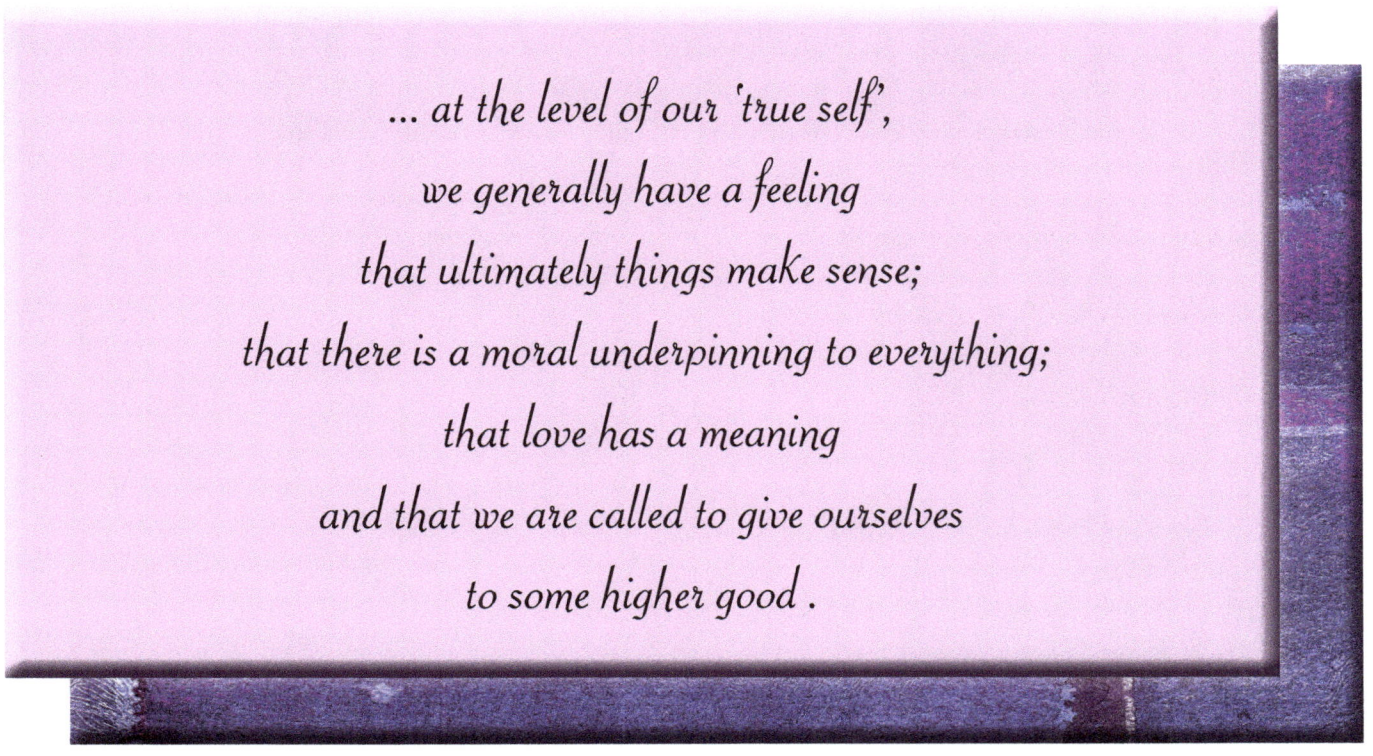

... at the level of our 'true self', we generally have a feeling that ultimately things make sense; that there is a moral underpinning to everything; that love has a meaning and that we are called to give ourselves to some higher good.

Holy Communion 51

Time for Thanksgiving
Taking time to reflect on the gift of life

In a sense, we each live in a world of our own making.

"We do not see things as *they* are," the Talmud explains, "we see them as *we* are." Our view of the world often depends on our emotional state, which in its turn depends on the habits of our mind and heart.

For some people, life is good, people are kind and beauty abounds. For others life is hard, people are cruel and beauty is a rarity. It becomes like looking at our own experience through a dirty window. There is no simple explanation for this difference in perception which exists between people undergoing similar experiences. Sometimes it is genetic, the way we were brought up to see the world, or some other aspect of personal development. Sometimes it defies logical analysis.

However, many believe it is related to that habit of mind associated with the human response of gratitude – the simple act of saying thanks.

At its core, the word 'Eucharist' simply means 'to give thanks'.

Like some silken thread, running through the prayers of the Mass, we are exhorted 'to give thanks'. The purpose of our coming together is repeated again and again.

But there is a time, after we receive Holy Communion, which is designed especially for us to draw within our own story and our own experience as a specific time for us to bring the power of gratitude to the surface of our minds. Brief though it sometimes is, the movement of the Mass allows some time and space for quiet reflection. It is to be jealously guarded. It is a time to quieten the racing mind, a time to give ourselves permission to slow the body and slow the brain.

The quiet mind appreciates the subtleties of life. The quiet mind finds satisfaction in simplicity. The small pleasures, the mundane tasks will become occasions for gratitude. Thankfulness arises from the quiet mind like dew settling on morning leaves. The cultivation of this habit of mind is central to the way we see our world, we see one another and we appreciate God's quiet presence in our experience.

Taking time to look into our inner world, the outer world makes more sense. The essence of belief and hope lie in the little things, the quiet moments. Those few moments after we have come out of our seat to receive the body and blood of the Risen Christ need to be carefully treasured. There is a deeply rooted need existing in every human heart – to give thanks. This is the time in the Mass when we especially feel the need to give thanks:

- for our faith, no matter how fragile or tentative.
- for being a tiny part of some vast river of believers from every village and city, every

Easter Creed

I believe that you can do new things.
Help my unbelief.

I believe that you can help us to make a way in the desert.
Help my unbelief.

I believe that you want to create rivers through the wasteland.
Help my unbelief.

I believe that we are not stuck to just repeat the evils of the past.
Help my unbelief.

I believe that I can do things that I was not able to do before.
Help my unbelief.

I believe that I might be able to forgive my enemy.
Help my unbelief.

I believe that peace among nations is possible.
Help my unbelief.

I believe that we can overcome the ways of violence.
Help my unbelief.

I believe that we can eliminate hunger and poverty.
Help my unbelief

I believe that we can overcome racism.
Help my unbelief.

I believe that we can create homes for everyone.
Help my unbelief.

I believe that we can finally drop the stones of condemnation.
Help my unbelief.

I believe that we will have a new heaven and a new earth.
Help my unbelief.

God, I believe that together we can do new things.
Help my unbelief.

Amen.

From *Pastoral Renewal Exchange*, no 89

culture, every language, the literate and illiterate, the hungry and the satisfied across this immense planet who join together in acknowledging their gracious and gentle God.

- for the people, the plants, the animals that have made our life possible and sustainable.
- for our body that constantly performs miracles of growth, transformation, protection and healing.
- for our food.
- for air, water, warmth, and for the awareness that the world is sustaining us in this moment.

Such simple thoughts are seeds that make us more human. Simple gratitude grows into compassion. Compassion and living in the subtle belief that we are all embraced in the gentle mystery of our God breeds the rich gift of human joy.

At our very best we are 'people of the Eucharist'.

His meals are harbingers of the banquet to be shared in the coming kingdom of God.

Did You Know

In the Gospel stories Jesus shares many meals

- In the Gospel descriptions of the meals Jesus shares, the expectations of his contemporaries are scandalously upset – he eats with misfits and outcasts, the unpopular and rejected, the handicapped and disenfranchised. They become examples of 'contagious holiness'.

- In about one-fifth of Luke's two books, the Gospel of Luke and The Acts of the Apostles, meals play a conspicuous role:

    a banquet at Levi's house. (Luke 5:27–39)

    a dinner at Simon the Pharisee's house (sinful woman). (Luke 7:36–50)

    breaking bread at Bethsaida. (Luke 9:10–17)

    hospitality at the house of Martha. (Luke 10:38–42)

    a noon meal at a Pharisee's house. (Luke 11:37–54)

    a Sabbath dinner at a Pharisee's house. (Luke 14:1–24)

    hospitality at the house of Zacchaeus. (Luke 19:1–10)

    breaking bread at the Passover meal. (Luke 22:7–38)

    breaking bread at Emmaus. (Luke 24:13–35)

    a supper with the disciples. (Luke 24:36–53)

- In these meal stories we learn important information about Jesus and the kingdom of God:

    Jesus is present, taking an active role whether as a guest or host. He is concerned about those at the table with him and serves them, responding to their need for food, healing, teaching or correction.

    He welcomes all, sinners and righteous, poor and rich. He does not fear being compromised by the company he keeps; and he overturns human expectations by expressing his own unique values.

    His meals are harbingers of the banquet to be shared in the coming kingdom of God.

    The light of Easter helps the Christian community understand the scriptures' witness to Jesus; the disciples recognise the Risen Lord in the breaking of the bread.

The Mass is ended – go in peace
The challenge to be a life-giver

Standing at the church door, the celebrant was making his best effort to farewell the stream of worshippers, hoping too that he would remember the names of most of them as they headed out of Sunday Mass in every direction.

Has this moment of worship changed anything? he mused. *Has this time of celebrating the Eucharist changed the way these people perceive their own lives, understand and respect the lives of others? Has it changed anything for me?*

The priest took some courage from a story he had read the night before. Talking about our ability to be changed and transformed, American educator Steven Covey related a simple story of how he personally was changed one morning when he was taking a commuter train to work.

The passengers were all sitting in their seats – some reading, others dozing, others contemplating with their eyes closed. A normal morning scene of peace and calm.

At one stop a man and three children entered the carriage. The children began yelling back and forth, throwing things, and even grabbing people's newspapers, thoroughly disturbing the entire carriage. And the father just sat there and did nothing.

It was not difficult to feel irritated. Covey admitted he couldn't believe the man's insensitivity in letting his children run wild in the carriage and doing nothing about it.

Clearly, everyone else in the carriage was also annoyed. Finally, Covey said, with all the patience he could muster, "Your children are really disturbing a lot of people. I wonder if you couldn't control them a little bit more?"

The man looked up as if coming into consciousness for the first time and said, "Oh, you are right. I can do something about it. You see, we have just come from the hospital where their mother died an hour ago. I don't know what to think and I suppose they don't know how to handle it either."

Covey was speechless.

Suddenly, he saw things differently. Because he saw differently, he felt differently. He behaved differently. His irritation vanished. He didn't have to worry about controlling his attitude or his behaviour. He felt sympathy for this man's pain. Feelings of compassion and sympathy flowed freely.

Nothing had changed in the carriage. The same people, the same irritation and the same kids. What had changed was a way of seeing it all and, with the seeing, a change of behaviour.

Change is possible, the priest once again reminded himself. The stream of worshippers hurried out, passing him with a greeting, off to the business and leisure of another Sunday. We *can* be changed! It happens all the time, more often than not quietly, almost imperceptibly, like the waves of the ocean gradually sculpting the sandstone cliff. We grow or we shrink.

When we grow new possibilities are born; we experience a deeper compassion for a broken world or for a fellow sufferer who is struggling. When we are called beyond the boundaries of ourselves, we come to an enhanced appreciation of the deep mystery of the human condition. We grow when we awaken to the belief that a gentle God is alive in every human heart, expressed in every culture and that this astonishing creation in which we exist shimmers with the miracle of divinity. Christians

*And so aware of
the mystery and wonder
we become speechless
before the joy in our hearts
and celebrate the sacredness of life
in the Eucharist.*

have a word for this change. It is called '*conversion*'.

But also, human change can be an experience of hardening our hearts. Life can shrink us. Sometimes it feels like we are drowning in a 'quick-fix, sugar-rush, attention-deficit' post-modern society. We can be driven by the worst compulsions of our disordered life, the insistent demands of our need to consume more and more of the world's diminishing resources, by our need to compete with and exploit others often weaker than ourselves, and by countless other so-called needs and wants that disfigure contemporary life. Christians have a name for this also. It is called simply '*sin*'.

The Mass itself, the church assures us, is a genuine act of reconciliation. Being present at the Eucharist, praying together as a community of faith, breaking the bread of the Eucharist with our fellow searchers, carries with it healing 'springs of living water' which promise new life for spirits which are parched.

Dominican priest Timothy Radcliffe points out that our worship together "is able by its very nature to touch some of the deepest springs of the human psyche and help us to free those sides of ourselves that we dare not face".

The celebration of the Eucharist is the church's ancient sacrament to help us see differently. If you see differently, you feel differently. If you feel differently, you act differently.

The contemporary believer lives between these two realities – we grow or we shrink. Life never allows us to tread water for long. Rarely does life-changing conversion strike as it did for Paul on the road to Damascus. More often, change comes like a gentle dawning, as our imagination awakens to a new sense of self, or it arrives by being set alight by someone else, seeing in us more than we have ever seen in ourselves, or by the utter beauty and courage of another. Many describe it as just that – an awakening.

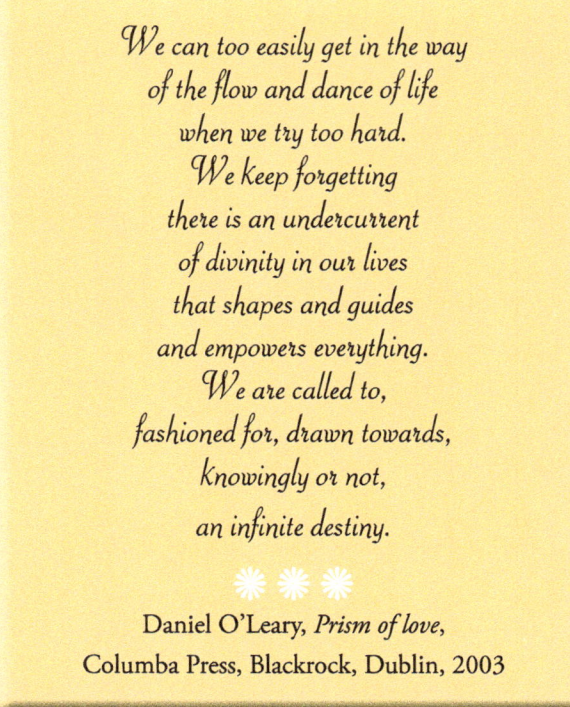

We can too easily get in the way of the flow and dance of life when we try too hard. We keep forgetting there is an undercurrent of divinity in our lives that shapes and guides and empowers everything. We are called to, fashioned for, drawn towards, knowingly or not, an infinite destiny.

❈ ❈ ❈

Daniel O'Leary, *Prism of love*, Columba Press, Blackrock, Dublin, 2003

The gospel, beyond any doubt, challenges us to act differently. Jesus was a life-giver. He enlivened all he met. The blind saw. The bed-ridden walked. The sick became well. All who met him with trust went away with an enhanced life.

To break the bread of the Eucharist within our simple parish communities challenges us to:

- reverence life in all of its sacredness
- challenge the blindness of a culture of narcissistic individualism
- act justly in an alarmingly unequal world, in which each day over 30,000 people die of hunger
- recognise and stand with the broken women and men who live on the margins in our own land
- accept the equality and special gifts of women in many cultures including our own
- act intelligently and commit ourselves to the prevention of the destruction of this fragile planet.

It is such actions as these that make us life-givers. If we see differently, we feel differently. If we feel differently, we act differently.

The priest wearily closes the church doors after the last parishioner has departed. On the wall of the vestibule he reflects on the framed words before him:

*We believe that the spirit of peace
is present with us in the church,
as we gather to celebrate our common existence,
the Resurrection of Jesus
and the fidelity of God.
And more deeply we believe
that in our struggle to love
we incarnate God in the world.
And so aware of the mystery and wonder
we become speechless before the joy in our hearts
and celebrate the sacredness of life in the Eucharist.*

With a small sigh, the minister of the Eucharist murmurs to himself, "And we can all say 'Amen' to that."

The truth of life
is that life is not a given.
We are its co-creators.
The globe is in our hands.
Life is at our mercy.
We must be impelled by the vision
that inspired it,
committed to the glory that created it,
and confident in the beauty
that sustains it.
To say "I believe" is to say that
my heart is in what I know
but do not know,
what I feel but cannot see,
what I want but do not have,
however much I have.
To say "I believe"
is to say yes
to the mystery of life.

Joan Chittister, *In search of belief*,
Harper Collins Publishers, Melbourne, 1999

The Eucharist in Scripture

In the writings of the New Testament, the words of the Last Supper are described in Paul's letter to the church in Corinth, and then in the Gospels of Luke, Matthew and Mark. The Acts of the Apostles describes the practice of the coming together of the early followers of the Risen Christ. Here are some of the descriptions found in the New Testament:

> For I received from the Lord what I also handed on to you, that the Lord Jesus, on the night he was handed over, took bread, and, after he had given thanks, broke it and said, "This is my body that is for you. Do this in remembrance of me." In the same way also the cup, after supper, saying, "This cup is the new covenant in my blood. Do this, as often as you drink it, in remembrance of me." For as often as you eat this bread and drink the cup, you proclaim the death of the Lord until he comes. (1 Corinthians 11:23–26)

> When the day of the Feast of Unleavened Bread arrived, the day of sacrificing the Passover lamb, he sent out Peter and John, instructing them, "Go and make preparations for us to eat the Passover…" They went…and prepared the Passover. When the hour came, he took his place at the table with his apostles. He said to them, "I have eagerly desired to eat this Passover with you before I suffer, for I tell you (that) from this time on I shall not eat the fruit of the vine until the kingdom of God comes." Then he took the bread, said the blessing, broke it, and gave it to them saying, "This is my body, which will be given for you; do this in memory of me." And likewise the cup after they had eaten, saying, "This cup is the new covenant in my blood, which will be shed for you. (Luke 22:7–20)

> On the first day of the feast of Unleavened Bread, the disciples approached Jesus and said, "Where do you want us to prepare for you to eat the Passover?…The disciples then did as Jesus had ordered, and prepared the Passover. When it was evening, he reclined at table with the Twelve…While they were eating, Jesus took bread, said the blessing, broke it, and giving it to his disciples said, "Take and eat; this is my body." Then he took a cup, gave thanks, and gave it to them saying, "Drink from it all of you, for this is my blood of the covenant, which will be shed on behalf of many for the forgiveness of sins." (Matthew 26:1–30)

It is important to note that in the idiom of Jesus' native tongue (Aramaic) the word 'many' asserts that it is not restricted to a chosen few. 'Many' in no way implies that Jesus' offering of himself is not for all.

> On the first day of the Feast of Unleavened Bread, when they sacrificed the Passover lamb, his disciples said to him, "Where do you want us to go and prepare for you to eat the Passover?"…The disciples then went off…and prepared the Passover… While they were eating, he took bread, said the blessing, broke it, and gave it to them, and said, "Take it: this is my body." Then he took a cup, gave thanks, and gave it to them, and they all drank from it. He said to them, "This is my blood of the covenant which will be shed for many…" (Mark 14:12–24)

> They devoted themselves to the teaching of the apostles and to the communal life, to the breaking of the bread and to the prayers… Every day they devoted themselves to eating together in the temple area and to breaking bread in their homes. They ate their meals with exultation and sincerity of heart, praising God and enjoying favour with all the people. And every day the Lord added to their number those who were being saved. (Acts 2:42, 46)

To know and to serve God, of course,
is why we are here,
a clear truth, that, like the nose on your face,
is near at hand and easily discernible
but can make you dizzy if you try to
focus on it hard,
but a little faith will see you through.
What else will do except faith in such
a cynical, corrupt time?
When the country goes temporarily to the dogs,
cats must learn to be circumspect, walk on fences,
sleep in trees, and have faith that
all this woofing is not the last word.
Gentleness is everywhere in daily life,
a sign that faith rules through ordinary things:
cooking and small talk,
through storytelling and making love, fishing,
tending animals and sweet corn and flowers,
through sports, music and books, raising kids
— all the places where the gravy soaks in
and grace shines through.

Garrison Keilor, *We are still married*, Viking Penguin, New York, 1990

Music in the Mass

St Augustine, who lived in Africa in the fourth century, said about singing hymns, "If you sing, you pray twice." The Christian churches use music to sing or chant prayers or as a listening experience. Many great composers, for example, Bach, Beethoven, Mozart, Monteverdi, Haydn, Tallis, Palestrina, Mahler, Handel and Bizet have written settings for the Mass, great hymns or great religious music. In the twentieth century, fine hymns have been written by composers such as John Tavener in England and Richard Connolly in Australia. In the Orthodox, Anglican and Catholic churches there are age-old chants especially for The Psalms.

From the beginning of Christianity, copying the example of Judaism from which sung prayers grew, poets have written the words for hymns that Christians use as prayers. Beside the hymns in the Bible, like the "Magnificat" and the "Benedictus", writers such as St Ephrem, Dante, Thomas Aquinas, Bernard of Clairvaux, Martin Luther, John Henry Newman, Charles and John Wesley, Ronald Knox, James McAuley, Bede the Venerable and John Donne have written words for hymns.

There are really good, easy-to-sing chants that come from Taize, the monastery in France where for sixty years many young adults have gone to pray and reflect and share community.

Abridged from Graham English, *Saying hello to God*, Melbourne, John Garratt Publishing, 2006

Catechism of the Catholic Church — texts

The Eucharist is the heart and the summit of the Church's life, for in it Christ associates his Church and all her members with his sacrifice of praise and thanksgiving offered once for all on the cross to his Father; by this sacrifice he pours out the graces of salvation on his Body which is the Church.

Catholic Catechism, Paragraph # 1407

The Eucharistic celebration always includes: the proclamation of the Word of God; thanksgiving to God the Father for all his benefits, above all the gift of his Son; the consecration of bread and wine; and participation in the liturgical banquet by receiving the Lord's body and blood. These elements constitute one single act of worship.

Catholic Catechism, Paragraph # 1408

The Eucharist is the memorial of Christ's Passover, that is, of the work of salvation accomplished by the life, death and resurrection of Christ, a work made present by the liturgical action.

Catholic Catechism, Paragraph # 1409

And yet the poetry of this age-old Catholic faith of ours
holds the belief that we are immersed in mystery,
that our lives are more than they seem,
that we belong to each other
and to a swirling universe whose energy resides
in an ever-present, creator God.

www.ingramcontent.com/pod-product-compliance
Lightning Source LLC
Chambersburg PA
CBHW061058170426
43199CB00025B/2934